D1736634

Testimony to the EXiles

Testimony to the Exiles

Sermons for GenXers and Other Postmoderns

Mark R. Feldmeir

CHALICE
PRESS
ST. LOUIS, MISSOURI

Cover and interior design: Elizabeth Wright

This book is printed on acid-free, recycled paper.

Visit Chalice Press on the World Wide Web at
www.chalicepress.com

10 9 8 7 6 5 4 3 2 1 03 04 05 06 07 08

Library of Congress Cataloging-in-Publication Data

(Pending)

Printed in the United States of America

Contents

Introduction

When it comes to the perilous task of preaching, I take to heart the earnest advice of Annie Dillard, who instructs her writing students to approach their craft as if they were dying, as if their audience consisted solely of terminal patients. "What would you begin writing if you knew you would die soon? What could you say to a dying person that would not enrage by its triviality?"[1]

Each week I stand before the three hundred souls of Santa Margarita United Methodist Church and dare to eschew the triviality that so many of my generation have come to expect, and have since rejected, from the North American church. I worship with people whose lives are far from trivial, whose needs and passions and hopes and aches are palpably real and infinitely meaningful. Together we come to worship to unpack our hopes and dreams, our grief, disbelief, disillusionment, betrayals, loneliness, and self-absorption, and trust that in that moment God will have something to say to us, something truthful that will in some measure help us to live more truthfully in the world.

My congregation has learned over the years that worship is, among other things, an act of telling the truth before God—the truth about our lives, the truth about our culture, the truth about the liberating gospel of Jesus Christ. We take up the task of the terminal and prepare to come clean, to strip down, to unearth what has been concealed, "to work," as Anne Truitt once said, "steadfastly along the nerve of one's own most intimate sensitivity." In moments of grace, I succeed at this as a preacher; more often than I'd care to admit, I fall short of the goal. But when it happens, when we tell the truth about ourselves, we are more apt than not to encounter the Truth that transcends even the most truthful realities of our lives.

Preachers, however, must move mountains in their own lives if they are to succeed at such a calling, because preachers have learned through practice to lie with careful yet subtle precision. In our preaching we too often tiptoe through the tithers, speaking in only partial truths, surrendering the radical, uncontainable gospel to self-help pop psychology, the reason of Enlightenment, the quest for relevancy, and the rational resolution of our private, individualistic problems. When we do that, Jesus starts to look more like Leo Buscaglia than "the way, the truth, and the life"; worship feels more like a Tony Robbins workshop on life planning than an act of praise and an encounter with mystery; the sacraments of baptism and eucharist, in the absence of honest confession and genuine repentance, become little more than spiritual Botox, with little enduring, transforming consequence; and mission, our "great commission," is reduced to the ABCs of so-called successful ministry: attendance, buildings, and cash. We de-scandalize the penetrating, terrifying truth of the gospel and simultaneously wonder why, for the terminal, for those to whom we preach, it's perceived as pure triviality—Christian karaoke in a post-Christian, disinterested world.

Each week I find that I must confess to God that it's not in my nature to want to tell the truth, not in the nature of my people to want to hear it. Then I sit down, open the good book, and wait for God to send in the wrecking ball and bulldozers to level the expectations, fears, insecurities, and disbelief that I have spent the better part of my life building and occupying with some degree of success and pride. Out of the rubble that remains, I poke around for evidence of good news, the truth, grace, God's very presence. Sometimes it's elusive, demanding to be sought out with greater diligence over several days; sometimes it relents and offers itself freely, immediately. Whatever it is I find there, I spread it out before me, as stones for a foundation; then I reach for the tools of my trade—story, imagination, conversations, art, culture, experience, tradition, to name a few—and get to work building what will inevitably be razed by God only moments after it is completed in the preaching event. On Monday, facing another blank page, I start over.

Doing this week in and week out can either make you crazy or make you honest; in my case, I suppose it does a little of both. As Anne Lamott once said, "My mind is a bad neighborhood I try not to go into alone." I like to think that on my best days, and especially on my worst days, I've got a companion in the One who promises to go with me, even to the ends of the world.

I am one among many preachers and ministers of my generation who take seriously the unequivocal yearning for spiritual experience and the undeniable suspicion of organized religion among my peers. While my audience is multigenerational, I speak with particularity to them—the exiles of the X Generation who have in large numbers checked out of organized religion in search of something more honest and less disconnected from the realities of life. In preaching among the exiles, I believe that the *suffering* of my generation can be redemptive if the church will allow it to be named and blessed by the One who deals in blessings. I believe that the *ambiguity and irony* that my generation so freely embraces must be honored as holy and honest, even as Jesus honors the despairing father in Mark's gospel who confesses, "Lord, I believe; help my unbelief." I believe that the *loneliness* of my generation is met by the One who no longer calls us *slaves, but friends.* And I believe that the *spiritual hunger* of my generation can be satisfied by the One who teaches us how to pray for "daily bread" (*com-panis,* "with friends").[2]

This in no way implies that I live out my vocation as a preacher by standing outside the circle of the saints who have gone before me. On the contrary, I find myself continually returning to the thoughtful, imaginative work of my elders: Barbara Brown Taylor, Frederick Buechner, Will Willimon, Len Sweet, Fred Craddock, Walter Brueggemann, to name a few. But I also am drawn to the truth that is told outside the walls of the church—the truth that is often told with greater clarity and honesty than few preachers today dare entertain. Weekly, I venture out of the ghetto and into the world of pop music, major motion pictures, literature, the arts, coffee house dialogues, the Internet. What I discover out there is a culture teeming with religious, spiritual intonations that intersect with both the gospel and the particular context in which I do ministry. Not all of it leads to the hope and truth we seek; in fact, much of it mocks the church's often suffocating, self-serving claims to authority and truth. But inasmuch as it strips us down and exposes our vulnerabilities, our lies, our myths, our blindness, it becomes a useful tool for forming an authentic, honest, indigenous proclamation of the gospel in our day.

What you will find in the pages that follow are sermons and worship ideas that have emerged from my work in the sacred laboratory of Santa Margarita United Methodist Church over the last several years. These sermons have a shelf life of a preheated TV dinner, which means that you may need to add plenty of your own salt to make them even remotely palatable. My hope in sharing them is that you will read them as one looking over the shoulder of another who, like you, struggles weekly to find God in the rubble of life, and struggles even more to find meaning in it. My hope is that you will not so much go and do likewise, but rather go and do otherwise, as Len Sweet suggests, in your own context, in your own community, which demands, among other things, that you tell the truth.

A few important notes merit your attention before reading on. First, where other published works have been quoted, it is important to note that I do not attribute any religious or spiritual intentions or motivations to the artists, writers, or producers of such material. A postmodern hermeneutic calls for an appreciation of the polyvalence of biblical and cultural narratives; there is more than one way to read a text. In quoting or referencing movies, song lyrics, poetry, and literature, I offer my own theological interpretation, which may or may not be the intention of the original artist.

Second, because of copyright restrictions, I am unable here to quote song lyrics without permission from the copyright holders. Where I was able to secure such permissions, the lyrics have been printed in full or partial form. In most cases, however, you will be provided a brief synopsis of or reference to the song, and you are encouraged to locate and explore the lyrics to the song on your own.

Practical Application of the Art Gallery

Each sermon in this volume includes a collection of artistic material intended to support and strengthen the central theme of the message, such as suggestions for film clips, poetry, prayers, secular music, literature, and "man on the street" interviews. In some cases, I have given specific recommendations on when and where to use this material in the worship service; more often than not, however, the preacher is encouraged to consider his or her own particular context for the most effective way to weave such material into the worship experience. I offer here a few suggestions:

Major Motion Picture Clips

I treat the use of movie clips as I do any other illustration within the body of the sermon, which means that if I have to explain it after I have used it, I've most likely illustrated the film rather than the gospel. Some people will "get it"; some may not. But my preference is almost always to be less literal and predictable and more allegorical with the clips I use; a clip should always point beyond itself. Be mindful that most postmoderns visit the local theater more often than they attend church; they are already well-trained to perceive their world as a series of scenes and can exegete a scene with great savvy and depth.

Typically, a brief, general synopsis of the film is necessary to set up the particular scene; the longer the synopsis, the more distracting the clip will be for your hearers. As a general rule, you should be able to introduce both the film and the clip in no more than five sentences. Providing your audiovisual team with a manuscript of your sermon and indicating clearly when you intend to use the clip will make the use of the clip more seamless and less obtrusive.

If possible, limit the clip to three minutes or less. Use no more than one clip in a sermon unless using a second clip from the same film (see "To Infinity and Beyond" for a rare example of this). Because a clip serves as an illustration, it can appear at any point in the sermon. Dimming the house lights before the clip will help draw the attention of the congregation to the screen; restoring the lighting will help draw the attention back to you.

When using film clips, be sensitive to issues of language, violence, and genre. Know your audience, know the film, and honor the sacred time and space of worship. If the clip cannot be edited or muted to accomplish this purpose, consider a more faithful alternative.

All recommended clips in this book are listed in VHS format, as many are not yet available on DVD. The "trademark" slide (i.e., *"Paramount Pictures")* at the beginning of each film is used as the starting point *(00:00)* for the suggested time settings of the recommended clips.

"Man on the Street"

Interviewing people on the street, at the local mall, or in your congregation can be a powerful method for communicating the needs, dreams, struggles, and joys of the people. Providing our listeners with an opportunity to share and hear their own stories creates a dialogue that is otherwise overlooked and unattainable in most of our preaching. A carefully planned preaching schedule will provide ample time for your video team to capture, edit, and produce a brief clip of interviews that can be introduced before or during the delivery of the sermon. Develop a simple question such as, "If you were about to become a refugee and could only pack three items, what would you pack?" (see "Daily Bread"). Limit your clip to two minutes or less, with careful attention to honesty, humor, and relevance, and show the clip at an appropriate time in the sermon.

Pop Music

Secular pop music, more than any other artistic medium, reveals the cultural narratives of a particular generation. Songs tell stories—about struggles, love, loneliness, regrets, fears, faith, hopes, and passions. Preachers would do well to exegete the lyrics to the songs their people hear for the many spiritual intonations found therein. Look for opportunities to connect a familiar song to your theme, and consider projecting lyrics while they are read or performed during worship. By naming the sacred in the secular in faithful ways, we can attach a depth of meaning to a song that, when heard later, reinforces the message we have proclaimed.

Poetry/Literature/Prayers

In this book, I have provided thematically relevant poetry to be either read, projected on the screen before worship, or printed in worship materials. In addition, I have occasionally provided selections from classical literature and prayers to be used for personal reflection. Each week my congregation publishes a "24/7 Guide" for worshipers to take home and use for devotional purposes throughout the week. This guide includes the scripture readings for Sunday, a daily lectionary for the week, a daily guide for personal prayer, opportunities for mission and service, and a "testimonial" (either literature, poetry, or a written reflection from members of the congregation).

Images

I have made general recommendations for the use of thematic images to be projected on the screen or published in worship bulletins. Consider recruiting a graphic artist in your congregation to integrate sermon titles, pictures, and images for use as title slides, background slides for song lyrics, and slides to be displayed during the sermon. In my congregation, this art is also published on the church Web site one week in advance, along with a sermon "teaser" to inform and prepare the congregation for the forthcoming Sunday.

I am grateful to the saints of Santa Margarita United Methodist Church, whose resilience and tenacity have proven triviality in the local church intolerable; to my friend and colleague Bill Johnson, whose imaginative sparks appear often in the pages of this book; to my early mentor Charles Simmons, who taught me that good preachers are avid readers of literature and culture; to Cal and Ann Shores for generously providing me a place to complete this book; and to Dr. David Polk of Chalice Press, who believed in the project and gave me a shot.

Above all I am grateful to my wife, Lori, whose companionship, humor, and honesty are the cherished sacramentals of our marriage; to Alyson, through whose imaginative eyes I see the world; and to Casey, whose amazing fall into the arms of grace reminds me daily that *the truth is out there.*

From Shame to Sheep

John 10:11–18

"I am the good shepherd. The good shepherd lays down his life for the sheep." (John 10:11)

Atari. *Friday Night Videos*. PacMan and Space Invaders. *Star Wars* and Prop. 13 and Pop Rocks and *The Day After. Ferris Bueller* and the Brat Pack and the ABC *After School Special*. The space shuttle Challenger, Farrah Fawcett, *The Breakfast Club, The Electric Company,* and *School House Rock. The Partridge Family,* Commodore 64, Rick Springfield, Journey, and Air Supply.

If you happened to be born between the years 1961 and 1980, you have been given a rather peculiar designation by your elders. You are among seventy-five million other Americans who are known, curiously, as Generation X. Your predecessors are known as Boomers, and before them, the Silent Generation, and before them, the G.I. Generation. We are the thirteenth American generation, known simply as X—the X signifying the mathematical symbol for the unknown. And we are, in a very real sense, an unknown. Other than our Xer peers, there were very few people in our lives who took the time to get to know us.

Studies show that 55 percent of us grew up in broken families; 20 percent of us were raised solely by our mothers; 35 percent of us grew up as latchkey kids; 20 percent of us grew up in poverty. Unlike the Boomer generation that preceded us, and the Millennial or Y generation that came after us, we became a generation that no one knew quite what to do with.

In 1975, nationally syndicated columnist Ann Landers conducted a poll in which she asked parents the question, "If you could go back and do it all over again, would you have children?" The question alone was revealing enough; then you look at the more than 50,000 responses, 70 percent of which said "No," and you see that X not only stood for unknown but also, for many of our generation, for unwanted.

Roe v. *Wade* and the national campaign for Zero Population Growth took care of some of that; 30 percent of our generation was aborted. But among those of us who saw the light of day, we still faced incredible odds: We were four times more likely to be incarcerated than the previous generation, three times more likely to run away from home, thirty times more likely to be institutionalized in a mental hospital, and three times more likely to take our own life.[1]

We were the first generation to be computer literate, and so we were the first to read that peculiar message that appeared on our monitors whenever we had disk failure on our PCs: *Abort, Retry, Ignore, Fail.* It's been said that there are no more palpable words to describe the experience and plight of Generation X than those four words. *Abort, Retry, Ignore, Fail.*[2]

Everclear, in their hit song, "Wonderful," sing about the disillusionment and abandonment that many of my generation feel, as well as the denial that lies beneath our experience.

It's a song about a young child whose home has become an emotional battlefield where parents scream and fight and later make promises they cannot keep and the child cannot understand. At the end of the school day, he dreads the prospect of returning home and fakes a smile to avoid questions. To make his not-so-wonderful life disappear, he closes his eyes and dreams of angels who console him with promises of a wonderful life—someday. As the child longs for *someday* he asks for honesty and understanding about his life today—*please don't tell me everything is wonderful now.*

We are a generation without a shepherd. We are a generation that seeks to belong to someone because we've never really belonged to anything or anyone; we are a seemingly lost generation because there haven't been many in our lives who took the time to lead us, or find us; we are an unknown generation because not many have taken the time to know us as anything other than X.

So if there is any passage in all of scripture that can speak to shame and loneliness felt by our generation, it is this one from the gospel of John. It is Jesus, standing in the midst of his lost and forlorn sheep, saying, "I am the good shepherd. The good shepherd lays down his life for the sheep. The hired hand, who is not the shepherd...sees the wolf coming and leaves the sheep and runs away—and the wolf snatches them and scatters them...[But] I am the good shepherd. I know my own and my own know me" (Jn. 10:11–12, 14).

From shame into sheep we are transformed by Jesus Christ. We are brought into a new family where we are known, where the hairs on our head are counted, where we matter so much that even if one of us wanders off at sunset, the Shepherd will come looking for us until he finds us and brings us back into the fold.

David Hilfiker serves as a doctor in downtown Washington, D.C. After practicing traditional medicine in the Midwest for several years, Hilfiker and his young family moved to D.C.'s inner city to practice what he now calls "poverty medicine." In the late 1980s he and others founded Christ House, a medical residence facility for the poor and the addicted who have been denied treatment by area hospitals. He wrote a book entitled *Not All of Us Are Saints,* in which he describes the difficulties and struggles of practicing poverty medicine; he writes of his seeming failure to make much of a difference and offers honest stories about how many of his patients return to the streets and to their addictions to drugs and alcohol.

In a moving story, he tells of a homeless alcoholic man named Clint with whom he had worked for more than a year in detox treatment. Clint's liver had been devastated by a lifetime of drinking; he was near death when he entered Christ House. After a few months of physical recovery and sobriety, Hilfiker thought Clint had made it. He was released to a halfway house, assigned to daily psychotherapy, admitted to Alcoholics Anonymous, but tragically returned to the streets and began drinking again. Over and over again, Clint would return to Hilfiker; but repeatedly, Clint would fail to make it. Each time, he was closer to death, and each time Hilfiker's heart was more deeply broken. Despite his best efforts, he had failed to heal Clint. He finally proposed alternative treatments, which Clint denied during his final relapse; he never saw Clint again.

Until months later, when he ran into him on a street corner near Christ House. He learned that Clint had been sober for several weeks, and though he wasn't sure he'd make it this time either, he landed a job, found a small apartment, attended daily AA meetings, and began dealing with the rage he'd been carrying around for years. Hilfiker invited Clint to attend the worship services at Christ House, which he did for several weeks.

One Sunday morning, without Hilfiker's knowledge, the pastor at Christ House invited Clint to serve communion at the worship service. As the people came forward to receive the sacraments, Hilfiker writes,

> I try to reflect on the meaning of the Eucharist, but my attention focuses on Clint and the stone chalice in those dark, weathered hands. As I step toward him I look up, and he suddenly grins, a broad beaming smile, almost a laugh. Perhaps embarrassed, he catches himself and solemnly offers the cup of communion, the laughter only in his eyes. "This is the blood of Jesus," he says, and I feel something crack within: all my awareness of the room and the other people and the hymn disappears. My vision blurs with tears, and I can feel my throat tightening. I give the chalice back and try to return his gaze, but I can't keep back the tears spilling down my cheeks...
>
> The light covered by childhood abuse and drowned for so many years by alcohol has flickered and is now burning. I was Clint's companion on an important part of his journey, and I do not understand why he is even alive.[3]

That's what this Good Shepherd does. Some of us wander off to nowhere; some of us get left in the middle of nowhere; some of us get chased out to nowhere; and some of us may even feel like nowhere is all we've ever known. But Jesus stands among us out in the middle of nowhere and says, "You are my sheep now. I'm your shepherd. I know everything about you and I still came looking for you. And now I want you to know everything about me."

Someone told me not long ago that she was beginning to think she'd wandered so far away from God that she wasn't sure God knew her forwarding address. She could have come right off the pages of the New Testament for all I knew, because the gospels are filled with people like her. A woman is caught in adultery, and just as the wolves gathered around her one afternoon, Jesus picks her up and says, "You are forgiven, go and sin no more." A tax collector by the name of Zacchaeus is the resident schmuck of the city, and Jesus spots him hiding in a sycamore tree and says, "I can make sheep out of schmucks. Let's go have lunch." A Samaritan woman who knows nothing but shame and scorn for living on the wrong side of the tracks bumps into Jesus at a well, and moments later she's telling the entire village that she met someone who knows everything about her and loves her still. Even a criminal pinned to a cross next to Jesus, a man who'd wandered so far away from God that he had no illusions that he'd even be able to sneak through the back door of heaven, even he, in all of his guilt and shame, is pulled into the flock and hears the words, "Today you will be with me in paradise."

Charlene was a typical Xer in the youth group I served during my seminary days. She was adopted as an infant; her parents divorced during her junior high years; her mother was diagnosed with cancer in her junior year in high school; and her father was busy creating another family that didn't happen to include her. The youth group was all she had, and not everyone in the youth group was particularly gracious with Charlene because she had a serious chip on her shoulder. I remember the night her mother died; I was driving her home from the hospital that night and she looked at me and asked, "Who is going to take care of me now?"

It wasn't long after that night that Charlene disappeared. I never heard from her again until a couple of years ago, when she left a message for me with my mother, who still lived in the area. The message said simply, "Thanks for being there."

Maybe that's all we can say to this Good Shepherd when it's all said and done. "Thanks for being there." Gratitude for this presence, this promise, this peace that comes from living in the fold, which is enough to keep us coming back from all our wanderings to say to the shepherd, "Thanks for being there. Thanks for being here. Thanks for letting me in."

ART GALLERY

Major Motion Picture Clips

Good Will Hunting (1997) tells the story of a South Boston whiz kid, Will (Matt Damon), who elects to clean the halls of MIT rather than enter them to study, slacking his way through life as a janitor despite having all the intellectual tools of academic success. His natural ability to unravel complex equations attracts the attention of a professor who won't let him quit, a beautiful Harvard student who wants to save him, a sympathetic buddy who wants him to escape South Boston, and a counselor (Robin Williams) who encourages him and leads him to a dramatic transformation.

In this scene, Will's counselor, Sean, distinguishes between knowing about the world and truly living in the world without fear of vulnerability, love, and depth of experience. This scene points to some of the underlying themes of GenX culture, namely, living with ambiguity, irony, and weakness. *(VHS, 0:46:00–0:51:00) Total time: 5:00.*

Pop Music

Collective Soul, "Needs"

Vulnerable to the weaknesses around him and overwhelmed by the weight of the world, the narrator, with irony, confesses that he doesn't need anybody; instead, he "just needs to learn the depth or doubt of faith to fall into."

Bobby McFerrin, "The 23rd Psalm"

A creative, secure affirmation of a "maternal" shepherd—"I will dwell in her house forever, forever and ever."

R.E.M., "Everybody Hurts"

Sympathizing with our generation's acute sense of loneliness and its high rate of suicide, singer Michael Stipe offers a word of hope and promise, affirming that we can "take comfort in our friends," that the pain will pass.

Poetry

David Rosenberg, "Psalm 23"

The Lord is my shepherd
and keeps me from wanting
what I can't have

lush green grass is set
around me and crystal water
to graze by

there I revive with my soul
find the way that love makes
for his name and though I pass

through cities of pain, through death's living shadow
I'm not afraid to touch
to know what I am

your shepherd's staff is always there
to keep me calm
in my body

you set a table before me
in the presence of my enemies
you give me grace to speak

to quiet them
to be full with humanness
to be warm in my soul's lightness

to feel contact every day
in my hand and in my belly
love coming down to me

in the air of your name, Lord
in your house
in my life.[4]

Dietrich Bonhoeffer, "Who Am I?"

Who am I?...

Am I then really all that which other men tell of?
Or am I only what I know of myself,
restless and longing and sick, like a bird in a cage,
struggling for breath, as though hands were
compressing my throat,
yearning for colours, for flowers, for the voices of birds,
thirsting for words of kindness, for neighbourliness,
trembling with anger at despotisms and petty
humiliation,
tossing in expectation of great events,
powerlessly trembling for friends at an infinite distance,
weary and empty at praying, at thinking, at making,
faint, and ready to say farewell to it all?

Who am I? This or the other?
Am I one person today, and tomorrow another?
Am I both at once? A hypocrite before others,
and before myself a contemptibly woebegone weakling?
Or is something within me still like a beaten army,
fleeing in disorder from victory already achieved?

Who am I? They mock me, these lonely questions of
mine.
Whoever I am, thou knowest, O God, I am thine.[5]

Images

Movie posters from the 1970s and 1980s, album covers, photographs of cars from the same era.

Sheep, shepherds, pastoral settings.

Invite Xers in your congregation to submit embarrassing childhood photos, and create a collage for projection.

Get over It

Philippians 3:4b–16

Not that I have already obtained this or have already reached the goal; but I press on to make it my own, because Christ Jesus has made me his own. (Philippians 3:12)

In the spring of my freshman year in college I had this wild dream that I could become the subject of an inspirational Disney film about a would-be minister who became a professional baseball player. On paper, it seemed like a pretty inspiring story—a story about a seventeen-year-old kid who dreamed every day of his life that he would make it to the big leagues but one day had this unexpected, extraordinary moment in his life when God suddenly showed up, tapped him on the shoulder, and said, "You're going to be a minister." The kid thought about it for a while—thought about the fact that he would most likely never go very far in baseball anyway—and he told God that he would go along with his change in plans. So he went off to college to begin his long quest, but every day in the spring of that first year, as he made his way to class, he'd see the baseball team out on the field and breathe in the smell of fresh-cut grass and diamond dust and baseball dreams, and he wondered to himself, "What could have been..." He thought about that every day, for two months, until one day he gave in and finally pulled his old glove out of the duffle bag, found a kid who didn't make the cut for the college team, and started throwing the ball around. He threw that ball every day—a hundred pitches a day—for an entire month. And the kid threw harder than he ever imagined he could; and his washed-up catcher gradually convinced him to try out for a local traveling team, just for the heck of it, because you never know. Can you hear the soundtrack?

The kid caught a break, got the tryout with the traveling team, showed up on a Saturday morning, and was unhittable. Not a single batter could touch him. Fastballs, sliders, breaking balls—he had it all working for him. For one day. And when the coach gave the kid a uniform at the end of practice, he could hear the music, the soundtrack of his impossible dream. He was like the *Rookie,* only twenty years younger.

A week later he was on the mound. He came in with a 5–0 lead in the fifth inning on the hottest day of the summer. When he climbed on top of the mound, he wondered why all of a sudden it felt like he was holding an over-inflated volleyball in his hand. The sixty feet six inches to the plate suddenly felt like a mile and half across the ocean; his shoulder felt like a dirty, wet dishrag, his fingers like stiff baby carrots dipped in ranch dressing.

He took a deep breath. He prayed. He threw. And then he watched his first pitch clear the left field fence and hit the tile roof of a house across the street, or was it two streets over? It was a sound that made the music of his sentimental screenplay stutter and crash. And that wasn't the worst of it. He did a nice Stevie Wonder impression with his next fifteen pitches, to put it mildly. And the next pitch he threw, with the bases loaded, is still orbiting the surface of the earth sixteen years later, just like his wild, wily dream.

Disney never called. The coach, however, did. He told the kid one thing—actually, two things. First, he said, "Feldman, I'm going to need your uniform back by the end of the week," and I remember thinking to myself that there really was no way of saying something like that politely. Second, he said, "Go be a minister, and pitch the gospel instead of a baseball, because that," he said, "is what you were made to do."

I wish I could say I gave up baseball to become a minister, but the truth is that baseball gave up on me. I'm not one to say that it had to be that way, that it was somehow predestined. All I can say is that it helped me find my true passion in life; it closed one door and opened another to a life I never before imagined, but couldn't live without. And I have never looked back since.

I learned the hard truth that you can't press forward in your life if you're living a life of "what could have been." You can't give your best to the life in front of you if you're always looking back at what could have been. You have to get over yourself if you're going to find yourself, and sometimes God rips a fastball over the fence and makes the decision easy for us. But sometimes there is a greater sacrifice. Sometimes we have to give up and get over even our best in order to find the still more excellent way—the life worth living.

Take the apostle Paul, for example. In Philippians, he tells us something that should cause us to pause and pay attention to what God is up to in our lives. Paul is like the Barry Bonds of the religious world. The guy is the complete package, religiously. He tells us today, "If anyone has reason to brag about their stuff, I've got more reason. I had it all. From day one, God and I were tight. I was born from the tribe of Benjamin, I was circumcised on the eighth day, I was the Hebrew of Hebrews; when it came to the laws of God, I knew them all, and practiced them to the letter; when it came to righteousness, I was Exhibit A. I was *the* star among stars. And then I met Jesus Christ, and I gave all that away in exchange for serving him." Paul says, "I had to give up my very best in order to be the person I am today."

In other words, there was no reasonable, rational explanation for Paul to become a Christian. He didn't have a falling out with the local synagogue; he didn't have some terrible event in his life where he blew it and had to come back to God begging for mercy. He didn't wreck his marriage or lose his job or waste his life savings on eBay and end up broke. Paul wasn't a candidate for the Dr. Phil show. He had it all together. He had no reason to abandon what he had worked most of his life to achieve—the status, the character, the community, the privileges. He had it all. Then he threw it away. "Whatever gains I had," he says, "these I have come to regard as rubbish because of Christ. I gave them all away in order to know the surpassing value of Christ Jesus."

Paul gave his life to build the church, to make Christians out of ordinary people like you and me. And by the time he wrote this letter to the Philippians, he found himself in jail, awaiting trial, awaiting his execution. There were some people who looked at Paul, after he walked away from the kind of life he had, and they must have wondered, "What could have been?" People must have wondered about the things Paul could have had, the life he could have lived, the things he could have done with all that potential. Did he have to give it all away in order to know Jesus Christ? Couldn't he have kept all that *and* known Christ?

I wish I could say yes, but I know what Paul would say. Paul would say that when you meet Jesus Christ, something happens that makes you want to be more like him than the person you see in the mirror. You see something that puts everything else in perspective. Your plans change; much of what you once thought was important suddenly changes. Some of the things you once thought you couldn't live without suddenly seem trivial.

And it's not hard to put our finger on some of those things in our lives. When we're honest about it, our priorities start to look a little whacked out. I read a *Wall Street Journal* report last month that addressed the issue of how our lives have changed since September 11. It concluded that things haven't changed much, despite the fact that in the days following the attacks, we said to ourselves, *things will never be the same again.* Church attendance spiked on the Sunday after the tragedy; 75 percent of all Christians reported that they attended church that Sunday. One year later, the number of those same people who attended church dropped to 34 percent nationally. Meanwhile, all this talk about removing the "one nation, under God," language from our *Pledge of Allegiance* somehow bothers us, and I have to wonder about that, given the number of people who actually practice what they preach, according to the *WSJ* report. I'm all for one nation under God, don't get me wrong. It's just not true, when we consider the evidence—34 percent? It seems to me that if you want to live *under* God, you'd have to worship God, you'd have to make some sacrifices in order to get to know him.

Paul says that when you meet up with Jesus Christ, something changes. He's not some accessory that you add to your already successful lifestyle; he's not someone you try to squeeze into your schedule when you have the time, when it's convenient; he's not a sticky fish on the back of your Beemer; he's not a personal trainer to help you attain some level of spiritual fitness. He's a person that dwells in you. And in order for him to dwell in you, you have to make room for him by throwing away some stuff that you've worked so hard to achieve and acquire. In order to be like him, you have to consider who he was—the Son of the Living God, who had everything: wisdom from on high, power to heal, the full blessing of God, but who, instead of using it all to his advantage, gave it up instead, redemptively, so that we could receive it and be more like him. Paul wants us to know that if we want to be like Jesus, if we want him to dwell in us, something has to give.

Like Paul, I do not want you to think that I've got this figured out in my life. Lord knows I've got my issues. Like you, I worry about my life far more than I should—my mobility, my future, my retirement plan, my kids' college education, my career, my security, my health, my status, my image. I want to be a success; I want to leave my mark on this world; I want to be good-looking and have great abs and keep my hair when I grow old. I want all of that *and* I want Jesus to dwell in me; but the truth of the matter is, if I have all that, there's not much room left for Jesus to come in. There are a lot of hurdles in my life I still have to get over if I'm going to see this race to completion.

So please don't get me wrong—I don't have this stuff figured out any more than you do. But I'm the one designated among you to point to the One who did figure this out, and to proclaim that if you want to be like him, if you want to be like Jesus, you'll have to be a sell-out, like Paul, who came to a point in his life where he understood that he couldn't sift through everything he knew of Jesus Christ and leave behind what he didn't like, taking only what fit into his plans, his lifestyle, his successes. For Paul it was all of Jesus or none of Jesus; you're either running the race or watching from the sidelines. He couldn't train a little now and make up the rest some other day.

You know what that's like, don't you? Someday I'm going to get around to doing that; someday I'm going to make some changes in my life; someday I'm going to be more disciplined with prayer, with church, with my stewardship. Someday I'm going to ask that guy at the office how his chemo is going; someday I'm going to grow that seed in my soul; someday I'll change the oil. Paul doesn't have time for someday. He knows it may never come. He knows his days are numbered. He knows that all he has is today. And I'm the appointed one who is supposed to tell you that your days are numbered, too, that we are all terminal, and that there is no day but today to get over whatever hurdle is in your life, the good and the bad, and get on with the race that God has set before you. When you're living a life of someday, you're always living in the red.

Thursday night I worked late at the office. I pulled out at around 1:30 in the morning and made my way home. Heading down Antonio Parkway, I drove past a half dozen cars parked on the side of the road. There were a dozen or so teenagers huddled around a few lighted candles and a makeshift memorial. Something compelled me to pull to the side of the road and join this huddle of complete strangers. Standing amidst broken glass and broken hearts, I read the white poster board sign in silence.

The kid's name was James. "Tell me about James," I said, and they told me the story of how James died in a drunken driving accident Tuesday night. They told me that James was eighteen years old, that his friend, who was driving the car, survived the crash. They told me what kind of kid James was, and how they were dealing with it all. Some of them were crying. Some of them were angry. Some of them couldn't believe that their friend was dead. We talked for quite a while out there on the side of the road. Then one of the boys looked at me and said, "I wonder if he kissed his mom before he left the house." Eighteen years old, and he's pondering the mysteries of what is important in his life and the choices he makes. Eighteen years old, and he's catching a glimpse of eternity, and how close in time we are to it, but how far away we are from a life worthy of it.

Paul says that we don't have time to live in the red anymore, that there is one who is worthy of the best we have to offer him, and when we give it, we'll make room for him; and he will come and dwell in us, so that the things that he lives for become the things we live for, and the things that he gave himself for become the very things we give ourselves for, even the very best things we have. After all, he says, that's what Jesus gave—his time, his talents, his treasures; his body, his life, on a cross. Jesus didn't pick and choose.

Chariots of Fire is the story of Eric Liddell, a deeply committed Christian and a remarkable runner who reaches the Olympics and decides that he cannot run one of his scheduled races because it falls on a Sunday, the Sabbath of the Lord. It is the one thing he will not compromise. He is given the choice to run on Thursday instead—the day on which he is already scheduled to run two other races. He knows that running all three races on the same day may very well cost him the gold medal, but his life is guided by what dwells within, and he will not compromise that; it is a sacrifice he is willing to make, a hurdle in his life he is willing to get over. *(Show major motion picture clip.)*

Where does the power to run the race to completion come from? It comes from within. It is he in us. When we honor him, he honors us. And when we run this race of faith, we can feel God's pleasure.

And Paul says, "Don't get me wrong. I'm not there yet. But I'm trying. I'm giving this my best shot. I'm running this race. It hurts more than I ever imagined; I'm nearly out of breath. I look like I'm bonking here, I know, but I'm going to get there. I believe that, and I'm willing to dig even deeper to break the tape. I don't know when I'll get there, but there's no looking back, and there's no intermission. Today is all I have. Today I'm going to be like Jesus.

Call him crazy, call him obsessive, call him a radical who took his faith far too seriously. Call him what you will, but his real name was Paul, and in case you're mistaken—he *did* look a lot like Jesus.

ART GALLERY

Major Motion Picture Clips

Chariots of Fire (1981) is the Oscar Award–winning film, based on a true story, about two very different long-distance runners competing for Britain in the 1924 Paris Olympic Games. Eric Liddell, a Scottish missionary, is a devout Christian who sees victory as an opportunity to glorify God, while Harold Abrahams, a Jewish student from Cambridge, sees victory as an opportunity to challenge anti-Semitism and gain acceptance by Britain's elite. Together, their lives tell the story of athletic excellence and spiritual awakening in post–WWI Britain.

This scene captures Liddell's final, dramatic race in Paris, in which he wins gold after electing to run all three races on the same day. While running, his voice-over speaks of honoring God, finding the power within to run the race to completion, and feeling God's pleasure. *(VHS, 1:53:10–1:55:45) Total time: 2:35.*

Pop Music

Bruce Springsteen, "Glory Days"
Boston, "Don't Look Back"
Jennifer Knapp, "A Little More"

Images

Runners on a track, hurdles, a runner breaking the tape at the finish line.

How Not to Do the Right Thing (and Still Please God)

Matthew 1:18–25

Her husband Joseph, being a righteous man and unwilling to expose her to public disgrace, planned to dismiss her quietly. But just when he had resolved to do this, an angel of the Lord appeared to him in a dream and said, "Joseph, son of David, do not be afraid to take Mary as your wife, for the child conceived in her is from the Holy Spirit. She will bear a son, and you are to name him Jesus, for he will save his people from their sins."...When Joseph awoke from sleep, he did as the angel of the Lord commanded him; he took her as his wife, but had no marital relations with her until she had borne a son; and he named him Jesus. (Matthew 1:19–21, 24–25)

A man and a woman meet up in heaven one afternoon. They had met once in their earthly lives but never got together. Neither had ever married. But now that they were in heaven, they knew they were always meant for each other. They took Saint Peter aside and asked him, "Is it possible for people in heaven to get married?" Saint Peter looked at them and said, "I'm sorry, I've never heard of anyone in heaven wanting to get married. I'm afraid you'll have to talk to the Lord about that." They were then escorted by the guardian angels into the presence of the Lord, where they repeated the request. The Lord looked at them solemnly and said, "I tell you what, wait five years and if you still want to get married, come back and we will talk about it again." Well, five years went by, and the couple, still very much wanting to get married, came back. Again, the Lord said, "Please, you must wait another five years, and then I will consider your request." Finally, they came before the Lord the third time, ten years after their original request, and asked the Lord again. This time, the Lord answered, "Yes, you may marry—this Saturday at 2:00 p.m."

Well, the wedding went beautifully. But after just a few weeks they realized they had made a horrible mistake; it just wasn't working. So they made another appointment to see the Lord, this time to ask if they could get a divorce in heaven. When the Lord heard their request, he looked at them, shook his head in disbelief, and said, "Look, it took us ten years to find a preacher up here in heaven; do you have any idea how long it'll take to find a lawyer?"

Sometimes we make all these plans in life, and what happens? I'll tell you what happens sometimes. God laughs. You ever notice that? There are times in our lives when all the plans we make are, in a matter of moments, scattered in the wind.

There is so much talk in our culture these days about creating life plans, setting goals, charting a path, and sticking to it. We plan out our careers, our families, our retirement, our education, our vacations, even our funerals. We get it all figured out, and then we discover that things rarely work out the way we've planned them.

I heard a business expert on National Public Radio recently who noted that if you want to start a business, or if you want to survive in your small business, remember the "Law of Two." The Law of Two says that it will take you twice as much time as you think to ultimately succeed; it will take twice as much energy and twice as much as money than you're willing to invest. You'll sacrifice twice as much as you planned; you'll fail twice as much as you succeed; and your success will be twice as sweet as you dreamed it would be.

The Law of Two. It's not just true in the business world; it's true of life and faith. You've got to put in twice the effort, believe twice as much as you think you are able, trust God twice as much as you'd comfortably prefer, and expect to go twice as far as you've already gone. That's true, isn't it? It's the Law of Two.

Take a look at Joseph, and you'll see what I mean. Who is Joseph? Before this angel visits him in his dream, Joseph isn't much of a player in the grand scheme of things. Even today, two thousand years later, he doesn't get a whole lot of press. You can look him up in a Bible dictionary and see that he's barely a footnote in history.

We know he's a carpenter. We know he lived the lifestyle of the not so rich and famous. He punched the clock, paid his dues, did his job, and at the end of the day, he hung up his tools and settled in for the night. Day in and day out. It doesn't get any simpler than that, right? When he wasn't at the shop, he'd hang out with Mary, maybe hit the malls, catch a movie, maybe even take her to Downtown Disney on payday. Joseph had a simple life, a good life. Scripture says he did everything right; he was a righteous man, a man of faith, true to God. You get the feeling that he wanted nothing more than to marry his sweetheart and settle into their life together, like Ward and June Cleaver, build a family, build the perfect, Orange County suburban life.

Joseph had plans. Honorable plans. Not great, cosmic plans, but good plans. Then God showed up, and laughed.

Well, the news wasn't good. Mary was *already* pregnant, and Joseph wasn't the lucky guy. Couldn't be, wouldn't be, no possible way he even might be, and you'd figure that there was no possible way he could ever get over that fact. How could he? Being a religious man, there were provisions for this kind of awkward situation. He had a way out, right? It's in his Bible. If he wasn't the father of this child, he would have to pull the plug on the wedding plans; he'd have to dump her, then see to it that she be stoned to death. It's in the book, Deuteronomy 22:20–21; it's one of the rules. It's the right thing to do. It's right there in the Bible.

Every once in a while I see this bumper sticker on the back of a car. Maybe you've seen it. It says, "God said it, I believe it, that settles it." I appreciate the intention of that statement, but I've got to tell you that if you buy into that kind of thinking, you're going to have a tough time with this passage. Sometimes it's not that simple. And you know something? The whole history of the world would be different today had Joseph bought into that line.

Sometimes God changes the rules. I want you to hear that this morning, because that's apparently what God does in this story about Joseph. God shows up one night in the form of an angel, and the angel says, "Joseph, I know what the Bible says about this. I know it, because I wrote it. I know what I said back then, but this is what I'm saying to you right now. You will be this kid's father. You will not walk away from this."

It would be the biggest decision Joseph would ever have to make in his life. To *not* do the right thing, in order to please God; to chuck his plans in order for God to accomplish His plans.

Sometimes we hide behind the rules, don't we? I spoke recently with someone about his agonizing experience at a previous church over the issue of his sexual orientation. The elders of the church, upon discovering that he and his partner were gay, informed them that they would have to pack their bags and move on, despite their five-years-long relationship of total fidelity. The pastor later confessed that he was torn over the decision of the board, *but the rules are rules,* he said. The two of them, along with their adopted child, have since found a church home that values commitment, fidelity, and faithfulness to God more than rules and convention. I think it was Garrison Keillor who said that there comes a point when you have to "give up your good Christian life and follow Christ."

It's the Law of Two. For Joseph it would take twice as much faith, twice as much courage, twice as much trust, twice as much risk in order to be twice the person he ever dreamed he would be. That's life; that's faith. That's the Law of Two.

Life is a risk, isn't it? I was reading Larry Lauden's recent book *The Book of Risks*. This is great stuff. Lauden reminds us of the risks we face every day of our lives. Did you know that one in every 400 Americans are injured in bed, and that almost every other day an American dies falling out of bed? Life is a risk. For you men here this morning, you need to know that you have a one in 7,000 chance that in the course of a year, you will suffer from a "shaving injury" serious enough to require medical attention. You didn't know that, did you? Here's one for all of us: one in 6,500 Americans are injured by their toilets every year. That's a risk, right? Before you get dressed every morning, you should know that you run a one in 2,600 annual risk of being injured on a snap or a zipper or some other part of your clothing.[1] I don't really want to think about that, to tell you the truth. It all means that by the time you finally walk out the door in the morning, you've already beaten the odds, but you're not out of the woods—there are the risks of driving, the risks of walking, the risks of eating. Not major risks, right? Until you do them all at the same time. I've seen you do it. You drive, eat, drink coffee, shave, sleep, read the paper, apply makeup, and chat on your cell phone all at once. You defy the odds.

Life is a risk. And faith—the kind of faith that Joseph has—is a risk. Wayne Gretzky, the "Great One" of the hockey world, had it right when he said, "You miss 100 percent of the shots you never take." Joseph took the shot.

I want you this week to take a few shots, to practice in your life the Law of Two.

Find someone in your life who is half as whole as you are, and offer him twice as much love as he would expect from you.

Find someone who deserves half as much love as you've already shown her, and give her two times more.

Find someone who has worked twice as hard as you in this world and only come half as far, and give him twice the support he needs.

Find someone whose spiritual cup is at most only half-full, and pray for her two times a day, that God might give her a double blessing.

Forgive twice as much as you are willing; when you are angry, take *two* deep breaths instead of one; give half as much thought to yourself, so that you can give twice as much of yourself to the needs of the world. Give someone twice the benefit of the doubt. And when you make your offering this morning, feel free to put twice as much in the plate. *It's the Law of Two.*

Dads, give your kids twice as much of your time this week; moms, practice twice the patience; kids, try twice as hard to tell your parents twice as often that you love them twice as much as you've only half-heartedly shown.

The Law of Two doesn't come naturally, which is why I want you to try twice as hard to practice it. It produces a harvest of righteousness and peace. Tenfold, a hundredfold. The return on the investment grows exponentially.

Mary Ann Bird wrote a short story entitled "The Whisper Test." It is a true story from her own life.

> I grew up knowing I was different, and I hated it. I was born with a cleft palate, and when I started school, my classmates made it clear to me how I must look to others: a little girl with a misshapen lip, crooked nose, lopsided teeth and garbled speech.
>
> When schoolmates would ask, "What happened to your lip?" I'd tell them I'd fallen and cut it on a piece of glass. Somehow it seemed more acceptable to have suffered an accident than to have been born different. I was convinced that no one outside my family could love me.
>
> There was, however, a teacher in the second grade that we all adored—Mrs. Leonard by name. She was short, round, happy—a sparkling lady. Annually, we would have a hearing test. I was virtually deaf in one of my ears; but when I had taken the test in past years, I discovered that if

> I did not press my hand as tightly upon my ears as I was instructed to do, I could pass the test. Mrs. Leonard gave the test to everyone in the class, and finally it was my turn. I knew from past years that as we stood against the door and covered one ear, the teacher sitting at her desk would whisper something and we would have to repeat it back...things like, "The sky is blue" or "Do you have new shoes?" I waited there for those words which God must have put into her mouth, those seven words which changed my life. Mrs. Leonard said, in her whisper, "I wish you were my little girl."[2]

That's what the Law of Two looks like. It's the risk of going beyond the expected so that your life will count for twice as much. It's what Joseph did. It's what Jesus did. It's how to not do the right thing according to the standards of this world so that you can please your Father in Heaven.

ART GALLERY

Major Motion Picture Clips

Clip 1: *The Sandlot* (1993). Young Scotty Smalls moves to a new neighborhood and manages to make friends with the ball-playing kids at the local sandlot. Together the gang has a series of hilarious and touching adventures.

In this scene, Scotty finds himself in a major bind: He's used his father's autographed "Babe Ruth" ball at the sandlot, and the ball has been hit over the feared neighbor's fence, where the infamous "Beast" (a ferocious Saint Bernard) guards it. As they scheme and ultimately fail in their creative plans to recover the ball, Benny has a dream one night in which Babe Ruth appears and implores him to simply climb the fence and get the ball. The following day, Benny takes the risk, leaps the fence, and survives a close call with the dreaded Beast. A wonderful, playful scene, illustrating the risks we often have to take in life in order to overcome seemingly impossible odds. *(VHS, 1:14:51–1:21:33) Total time: 6:42.*

Clip 2: *Leap of Faith* (1993) is an *Elmer Gantry*–type film about the shyster preacher Rev. Jonas Nightengale (Steve Martin), who trades salvation and miracles for donations to his touring ministry. When his tour bus breaks down in an impoverished farm town, he learns a lesson about real miracles.

In this scene, Nightengale is spooked by an unplanned, unstaged healing of a crippled boy, which immediately inspires the entire town to greater devotion to God. Nightengale, however, knowing he had nothing to do with the miracle, faces a crossroads and, in the end, a miracle of his own. Confessing later to the healed boy that he's a fake and that his ministry is just a show for "suckers," the boy responds by asking, "What does it matter if you get the job done?" To which Nightengale replies, "Kid, it makes all the difference in the world." *(1:31:38–1:34:45) Total time: 3:07.*

Pop Music

U2, "All I Want Is You"

Of all the "promises" we make in our lives, of all the grand plans we fashion, of all the offerings we make, it all comes down to the unconditional, free gift of one's self, where true love and commitment is found.

Images

Photographs of risk, such as rock climbing, skydiving, hang gliding.

Images of twos or pairs, such as two fingers, two people, twins, the number 2, and so on.

Take the Long Way Home

Matthew 2:1–12

Having been warned in a dream not to return to Herod, they left for their own country by another road. (Matthew 2:12)

It is August 8, 1943. A man sits in a Berlin prison cell deep in intimate prayer and quite at peace with himself and God. On a table in front of him is a single piece of paper, a promise to serve in the Nazi medical corps. All he is required to do is sign his name, and the Nazis will spare his life.

It is a simple choice. His guards encourage him to sign the paper. His parish priest and bishop pray for him to sign it and save himself. His wife and three little girls beg him to give up and give in and sign the document so that one day he can come home. But Franz Jagerstatter will not sign the paper.

There were no compromises, no deals, no concessions. For Jagerstatter, it was the long way home, but the only way home. "There have always been heroes and martyrs who gave their lives—often in horrible ways—for Christ and their faith," he wrote. "If we hope to reach our goal some day, then we, too, must become heroes of the faith. For as long as we fear others more than God, we will never make the grade...The important thing is to fear God rather than people."

The following morning, Franz Jagerstatter, at the age of thirty-seven, took up his fear, made his solitary stand, and gave his heroic witness. After his execution, the chaplain declared that Franz "lived as a saint and died a hero. I say this with certainty that this simple man is the only saint that I have ever met in my lifetime."[1]

It happens, some time after we take down the lighted Santa from the rooftop and drag the dead Noble Fir out to the curb and bury the last fruitcake in the backyard, that we come face to face with what William Butler Yeats called, "the uncontrollable mystery on the bestial floor"[2]—this King of kings who saves us from the clutches of Herod's prisons and shows us the way home, if only we will consent.

Herod is mad as hell and scared to death. He's pacing the cold marble floors of his palace back in Jerusalem, waiting for us to return from our journey to Bethlehem, waiting for us to come back and tell him that our journey was made in vain, that the kid is no king at all, that there is no king like Herod. But Herod knows that there are at least two ways home, and one of those ways does not pass through Jerusalem. So tonight he's waiting and wondering which way we'll choose.

When the dust of Christmas finally settles in the dark stables of our souls, we have to ask ourselves, *Who owns us? Whose will we be now? Which road will we take home tonight; and if we choose the more excellent way, what then will we say to Herod when he comes knocking on our door to make his next deal?*

We may never face the Herod that Franz Jagerstatter faced more than fifty years ago, but in moments of rare honesty we confess a Herod in each of our lives that is equally fierce and persistent. While we like to think that we're as free as any generation has ever been before, here at the end of the most prosperous century in American history, we all carry around our own peculiar chains that keep us anchored to Herod.

The wars we wage with other people in our lives—listen, and you'll hear the rattling of Herod's chains; the denial about a certain sin that keeps us pinned and paralyzed—listen; the clinging to the past, or some past event, that we can neither forgive nor forget nor free ourselves from; the gossip, the cheap talk, the slander, the jokes at the water cooler—stop and listen; the bottle of Bushmill's, the dark chat rooms on the Internet at midnight, the excessive lifestyle we can neither afford nor justify nor resist. There has to be a way home that doesn't pass through Herod's palace.

The Pulitzer Prize–wining musical *Rent* is one of the most compelling social commentaries on Broadway. It's about my generation, the X generation; it's about the struggles, the faith, the brokenness, and all the Herods we face. It's about "Living in America" at the end of the millennium, where we are forced to play the frantic game of working ourselves to death while burying our hurts, our shame, our thoughts, our conscience for the sake of self-promotion and personal gain. *When you're living in America at the end of the millennium, you are what you own.*

It's the gospel according to Herod, isn't it? What we own—the physical, emotional, spiritual baggage—ends up, when it's all said and done, owning us.

I've been saving my personal bulk mail for the last three months. Not all of it, just the credit card solicitations. You get those, right? Look at the return address next time; you'll see Herod's name and address right there on the upper left-hand corner. It's been my personal mission to collect Herod's letters. In the last three months, I've collected forty-six of those solicitations from more than twenty different banks. They apparently *really* like me, right? They *really* want me; *really* want me to have everything I want, to do anything my free heart desires. So I've done the math on this. With all of those credit cards, I can buy $414,000 worth of stuff, at an average introductory interest rate of 2.9 percent for six months. It's the gospel according to Herod. Do you hear the chains rattling?

The problem with the freedom that Herod wants to give us is that it promises to get us what we want, but it doesn't give us a clue about what's really worth having. So there has to be a way home that doesn't pass through Herod's palace. But it is not the easy way home.

I like the apostle Paul's confession. Even Paul had his Herod. He confesses that he feels anything but free. "I do not understand my own actions. For I do not do what I want," he says, "but I do the very thing I hate" (Rom. 7:15). So he asks the question that we all find ourselves asking in moments of truth: "Who will rescue me from this body of death?" (v. 24).

And Jesus, this uncontrollable mystery, says, "I think I can help you with that." Surprisingly, it's not the answer we had ordered. Instead of offering us more freedom to do whatever we want to do, he says there is only one way home that we are truly free to take. He says, "You take the long way home, and I'll take the road to Jerusalem. I'll take on Herod."

Thomas Lynch is a writer, poet, and mortician in Michigan. In his recent book *Bodies in Motion and at Rest*, he tells the story about reaching a point in his life when he finally had to take the long way home. He writes about his chronic struggle with alcoholism, an illness that had been passed down from generation to generation in his family. He reached a point where he finally entered a program, returned to God, and sobered up; his life changed. He was a free man. But his high-school-age son was already well on his way to Herod's palace:

> It was autumn of his freshman year in high school—when his grades went to hell and his smile disappeared and the music in our house got dark, I took him out of school one morning and said I was taking him to find out what the matter was. I said I thought there must be something very wrong to account for all the changes I could see. Maybe a tumor or a loose screw or maybe, because it ran in our family, drink and drugs and addictions. I told him we wouldn't quit until we found out what accounted for the darkness that had descended on his life and times. No stone would be unturned.
>
> So we started with the drug and alcohol assessment, which turned up, unremarkably, positive. He was fourteen and trying anything that came his way...
>
> By midwinter things had gone from bad to worse. I tried my best to ignore the obvious—his lackluster grades, the long hours in his room, the distance he began to keep, the smell of alcohol that was always on him. One night he came home besotted and muddy. He had passed out in the park, in a puddle. How he kept from drowning, how he crawled home, remains a mystery. The next morning I took him to a treatment center...My son said if I made him go he'd kill himself. There was a calm in his voice that said he wasn't bluffing. I said he was killing himself already. I said I'd buried lots of boys for lots of fathers. I said if I was going to have to be like those poor hollow men, standing in the funeral home with my darling son in a casket, while neighbors and friends and family gathered to say they wished there was something they could say or do, I told him, if he was going to be dead either way, at least he wouldn't die of my denial, my ignorance, my unwillingness to deal with the way we are. I said if he killed himself I would miss him terribly. I would never forget him and always love him and I'd hate to outlive him but I'd survive. And I'd call someone before I'd drink about it.
>
> Calling this bet broke something inside.[3]

"Do not think that I have come to bring peace to the earth," says this Jesus. "I have not come to bring peace, but a sword" (Mt. 10:34). And this sword will break the chains that bind us, so that the way home doesn't have to pass through Herod's palace. And Herod will rage. The longer he waits for us, the more he will rage. Until the last chain drops, and we no longer fear him more than God. That's when we make the grade. That's when we know we've finally arrived at that place called *home*.

ART GALLERY

Major Motion Picture Clips

Clip 1: In the movie *Forrest Gump* (1994), the title character (Tom Hanks) leads viewers through an accidental travelogue of American social history from the early 1960s through the present in this revisionist fable. Vietnam, desegregation, Watergate, and more are presented from the perspective of Hanks's lovably slow-witted character as he finds himself embroiled in situations he can't quite comprehend.

In this clip, Forrest is on the run, literally. He's running from his past, running to numb the pain of his disappointment, and running because he has yet to find his "home" in the world. He runs for three years, two months, fourteen days and sixteen hours before finally deciding that he's had enough. In the desert, followed by dozens of inspired runners, Forrest decides his running days are over. *(VHS, 1:56:44–1:58:47) Total time: 2:03.*

Clip 2: *Good Will Hunting* (1997) tells the story of a South Boston whiz kid (Matt Damon) who elects to clean the halls of MIT rather than enter them to study, slacking his way through life as a janitor despite having all the intellectual tools of academic success. His natural ability to unravel complex equations attracts the attention of a professor who won't let him quit, a beautiful Harvard student who wants to save him, a sympathetic buddy who wants him to escape South Boston, and a counselor (Robin Williams) who encourages him and leads him to a dramatic transformation.

In this scene Will's counselor, Sean, leads Will to confront his painful past of having been physically abused by his father and helps Will to understand, "It's not your fault." This scene, one of the most compelling scenes on film in recent history, contains explicit language that may be inappropriate for worship; be prepared to edit or mute the sound, if necessary. *(VHS, 1:46:50–1:50:30) Total time: 4:40.*

"Man on the Street"

Interview people on the street, or in your congregation, seeking responses to the following question:

> If you could remove one obstacle in your personal life, what would it be?

Pop Music

Consider inviting your music team to perform U2's, "Walk On" as an anthem. Written by Bono, the song is dedicated to a Burmese academic from Oxford University, Aung San Suu Kyi, who took her courage into her hands and returned to Burma.

"She knew that she was going back to a country controlled by a brutal and oppressive regime and that her life and her freedom would be under threat. But inspired by the belief that only fighting—and defeating—fear can you truly be free, she became a leader of the National League for Democracy and spearheaded the campaign against the corrupt controlling military junta. "It was just one of the great acts of courage of the twentieth century," Bono reflects, "and it continues into the twenty-first."[4]

Aung San Suu Kyi was placed under house arrest in 1989. She was unable to receive visitors or communicate freely. But her witness became a powerful and enduring symbol of the fight for democratic rights in the face of totalitarianism. Kyi remained under house arrest until 1995, and her movements have subsequently been severely restricted.

Supertramp, "Take the Long Way Home"

Images

Roads, highways, desert landscapes, maps, and chains.

Incite Hope*

Isaiah 61:1–4, 10–11

They shall build up the ancient ruins, they shall raise up the former devastations; they shall repair the ruined cities, the devastations of many generations. (Isaiah 61:4)

A New York firefighter was captured on film shortly after the World Trade Center attacks Tuesday morning, covered in ash, exhausted, breathing with the aid of an oxygen mask. He was gearing up to go back into the rubble when the interviewer asked him in disbelief, "You're not going back in there are you?" To which the firefighter replied, "I have to go in there. It's my job."

We all have a job to do. We've come here today to listen to God, hoping that somewhere amid the rubble that fills our fractured souls we might hear the call. What is it that you must do today, in light of the tragic events of this week?

The prophet Isaiah walks among the rubble and ashes of his homeland, among the ruins and devastation of what once was the city of God, and he dares to proclaim to his people the good news above all other news—*God reigns.* The Babylonians have plundered Zion; his people have been lead out to slaughter and into slavery; those who survived had given up on God, given up on each other, given in to the powers that be. It doesn't look good.

But there is Isaiah, inciting hope, reminding them that this faithful remnant will rebuild the ruins, will rise above the former devastations, will be called oaks of righteousness, the planting of God. They will wear the robes of righteousness, the crown of salvation. They will be the living evidence that God reigns in the world, that the Babylonians have not triumphed.

*This sermon was preached on September 16, 2001.

The Babylonians took our buildings this week. They took our cities. They took thousands of our brothers and sisters. They took our sense of security. But they did not take our soul.

They did not take our soul. But the question that lies ahead of us, the question we have to answer in these days of uncertainty and anxiety, is one that only we can answer: Though they did not, could not, take our soul, will we so freely relinquish it?

I speak of soul, but I do not confuse soul with national spirit or patriotism. There is a time and place for national spirit; that time may indeed be today for you, but that place is not here, within these holy walls. We cannot surrender the gospel to the powers that be, to earthly kingdoms, no matter how high and honorable they are. Earthly kingdoms rise and fall; the kingdom of God endures forever. So today we hold up God and soul above country and national spirit. God will rebuild the ruins so that all nations might be drawn to him.

We have a job to do as Christians. It is to stand up in the midst of the city and proclaim that God reigns, that the one thing that has not been taken from us, that cannot be taken from us, is the soul of a people, which belongs to God because it comes from God. It can neither be bought nor sold nor taken from us by force. But I will tell you the truth—it *can* be given up, it *can* be surrendered, it *can* be lost to us, bartered for the idols of violence, revenge, and bloodshed.

We have a job to do. It is to incite hope in the city; to bring good news, as Isaiah says, to the oppressed; to bind up the brokenhearted; to proclaim liberty to the captives; and to announce that God reigns. To comfort the mourning, to give them a garland instead of ashes, the oil of gladness instead of mourning, the mantle of praise instead of a faint spirit. To wear the robe of God's righteousness, and to be found worthy of his crown of salvation.

To do that, you have to thirst for righteousness more than you thirst for blood; to do that you have to meet physical force with soul force; to do that you have to become the hands that build rather than those that destroy. And that is something we cannot do on our own. But we have this hope that it is something that God will do through us, if we do not surrender our souls to the gods of despair and hate.

It is too early for Americans to talk about forgiving the enemy. Less than a week after the attacks, we have yet to understand clearly who the enemy is, and to speak of forgiveness today would sound too much like acquiescence and blind pacifism. It is too early today to talk about that, though I will tell you that we will have to talk about that someday.

It is also too early, I believe, to talk about retaliation, principles of just war, nuclear bombs, and bloodshed. Our anger, though inevitable and palpably real, is arrogance; there is nothing righteous about it. Instead of raising our fists in protest this morning, we should be found on our knees mourning, grieving for the loss of life and for the potential loss of life in the days ahead.

So while there are some things we cannot bring ourselves to talk about today, I will tell you what we can talk about as Christians. We can talk about the need for spiritual purity; we can recognize our need to pray for forgiveness for ourselves, as strange and unpopular as that sounds; we can pray for pure intentions.

We are taught from birth to buy into what Walter Wink has labeled the myth of redemptive violence.[1] The myth of redemptive violence is played over and over again on television—from *Tom and Jerry* and *Batman and Robin* to the *Terminator* and *Diehard*. The myth maintains that justice is finally served and evil is finally defeated when the superhero breaks free and takes matters into his own hands, restoring order and peace, crushing the villain, through violent means.

It is believed that the average child watches 36,000 hours of television before his eighteenth birthday. During that time, he will witness 15,000 murders—some by villains, but the vast majority by those we call *superheroes.*

The myth of redemptive violence has become so much a part of the American psyche that we must at least confess it honestly before God and ask God if He would have any part of that. It has become so much a part of our lives that we are apt to use it perhaps more readily and with more pleasure than we ought. This is sin, and we need to confess that, to lay it before God and ask Him to judge it, to see whether God would find it worthy and honorable.

Is there another way for us today? Is there a better way? God only knows, which is why we must ask God for pure intentions and pure hearts today, freedom from hate, freedom from anger, freedom from our premature judgments, freedom from our natural hunger for vengeance.

A CBS poll yesterday (Saturday, September 15) found 68 percent of Americans said the United States should retaliate even if innocent people were killed; 60 percent supported such action even if "many thousands of civilians are killed." *God help us.*

Somewhere today there is an impoverished Afghani mother with children in the northern hills of her homeland, whose innocence is no less, whose value in life is no less, than the American mothers and fathers whose lives were cut down this week. We surrender our souls when we deny the truth of that. We surrender our souls to the gods of Babylon when we meet the forces of hate with hate, evil with evil. We only intensify the existence of genuine evil in the universe when we do that. "An eye for an eye," said Martin Luther King, Jr., "makes everyone blind."

So we pray to God for purity of heart and mind. We pray that God would show us the ways of justice and save us from careless violence.

Dietrich Bonhoeffer was a Lutheran pastor in Germany during the rise of Nazism. He was a resister in the Confessing Church movement; he was not a pacifist. Alleged to be involved in a failed attempt to assassinate Hitler, he served more than three years in Tegel prison before his eventual execution in a concentration camp at Flossenburg.

While he was in jail, he wrote prayers, papers, and letters, which were preserved and later published. The letters and papers express his utter disbelief in the powers of evil in the world; his anger, grief, sadness in knowing that millions of Jews were being carted into camps and gassed while the apathetic Christian world looked on. Less than a year before his execution, on Christmas morning, 1943, he wrote this prayer, which has become my prayer this week:

> O God, early in the morning I cry to you.
> Help me to pray.
> And to concentrate my thoughts on you;
> I cannot do this alone.
> In me there is darkness,
> But with you there is light;
> I am lonely, but you do not leave me;
> I am feeble in heart, but with you there is help;
> I am restless, but with you there is peace;
> In me there is bitterness, but with you there is peace;
> I do not understand your ways,
> But you know the way for me...

O Merciful God,
forgive me all the sins that I have committed
against you and against my fellow men.
I trust in your grace
and commit my life wholly into your hands.
Do with me according to your will
and as is best for me.
Whether I live or die, I am with you,
and you, my God, are with me.
Lord, I wait for your salvation
and for your kingdom.
Amen.[2]

That's the prayer of a man who longs for freedom from the gods of Babylon. A man who knows that the discernment of God's will begins with humble confession and the surrender of his own fragmented, tormented will.

Within a year of the writing of that prayer, Bonhoeffer was executed by hanging, shortly before the camps were liberated by American troops. But he died wearing the robe of righteousness, the crown of salvation. The Nazis took his life, but they couldn't take his soul.

So we pray for purity. We also pray for *unity,* for a total commitment to the kingdom vision that God yearns for, for freedom and liberty not only for Americans but also for all humanity. In the kingdom of God there is no division, no separation, no "us" and "them," no nationality.

A friend of mine was unable to leave Orlando all week; he couldn't get a flight until late Thursday. He told me that when he finally boarded the plane, he immediately noticed a man of Arab descent on board. He said he couldn't for the life of him take his eyes off the man. After some period of time, the stranger turned around and asked my friend, "Why are you staring at me?"

We need to confront and confess that suspicion within us, that distrust, that fear—all of which become the seeds of bigotry and hate. "There is...one Lord," says Paul, "one God and Father of all, who is above all and through all and in all" (Eph. 4:5–6).

Chief Seattle, the prophetic Native American voice of the nineteenth century, preached this better than most Christians of his day and of ours. *The United Methodist Book of Worship* includes a prayer inspired by his prophetic wisdom:

Every part of this earth is sacred.
Every shining pine needle, every sandy shore,
Every mist in the dark woods,
Every clearing and humming insect is holy.
The rocky crest, the meadow, the beast and all the people,
All belong to the same family.
Teach your children that the earth is our mother.
Whatever befalls the earth befalls the children of the earth.
We are part of the earth, and the earth is a part of us.
The rivers are our brothers, they quench our thirst.
The perfumed flowers are our sisters, the air is precious,
For all of us share the same breath.
The wind that gave our grandparents breath also receives their last sigh.
The wind gave our children the spirit of life.
This we know, the earth does not belong to us,
We belong to the earth.
This we know, all things are connected.
Like the blood that unites one family, all things are connected.
Our God is the same God, whose compassion is equal for all.
For we did not weave the web of life.
We are merely a stranger in it.
Whatever we do to the web we do to ourselves.[3]

Purity and unity. These are the things that make for peace, that incite hope, that rebuild the ruins. They are not things we can do on our own. These make for a tall order.

Our job is to incite hope, and in a world of despair and hopelessness, that is a tall order. Hope is not a feeling; hope is not an emotion; hope is the work we do, our vocation as Christians, and it takes all we have to do it faithfully.

Bono, the lead singer of the rock band U2, works daily, passionately, to end Third World debt and to end AIDS on the African continent. He was interviewed recently about why he does what he does. And he said, "I do believe that the Kingdom of Heaven is taken by force. God doesn't mind if we bang on the door to heaven sometimes, asking him to listen to what we have to say...At least, that's the kind of religion I believe in."[4]

I want to wear out that door to the kingdom. I want to bang on that door so often that God knows me on a first-name basis. I want God to get tired of me banging, asking him to use me to incite hope, until he just turns me around and points to where he wants me to start.

And I want you to go there with me. To incite hope, not hate. To incite hope, not despair. To utter the humble, yet confident confession that *God reigns.*

Incite hope, people of God. Put on the robe of righteousness, the crown of salvation, and rebuild the ruins. And the *peace* of God—Father, Son, and Holy Spirit—be with you, and above you, and before you always.

ART GALLERY

Major Motion Picture Clips

Patch Adams (1998), starring Robin Williams, is based on a true story of an aspiring medical student, Hunter "Patch" Adams, who, in the 1970s, attempts to treat his patients with a medicine that modern science has completely disregarded: humor and compassion. While his patients and fellow staff members appreciate his approach, the powers-that-be frown upon his "unschooled" methods and attempt to prevent him from practicing.

In this clip, Patch struggles to accept the tragic death of his closest friend and dares question the compassion and justice of God. The scene ends when a butterfly floats gracefully before him. *(VHS, 1:32:32–1:34:55) Total time: 2:23.*

Images

A dramatic slide presentation followed the preaching of this sermon. A total of fifty-one slides faded in and out, supported by a reflective musical selection (instrumental), using the following combination of scripture readings and photographs taken by news agencies throughout the week.

By the rivers of Babylon—
there we sat down and there we wept. (Ps. 137:1)

Images: Bystanders at ground zero, weeping and praying and holding one another.

Who will separate us from the love of God?

Image: A single photograph of firefighters carrying their fallen chaplain, the Reverend Mychal Judge, out of the rubble.

Will hardship, or distress, or persecution, or famine...or peril or sword?

Image: A single photograph of a lone man running through the street with a cloud of ash and smoke billowing behind him.

No, in all these things we are more than conquerors through him who loved us.

Image: A photograph of firefighters raising the American flag in a pile of rubble.

For I am convinced that neither death, nor life,
nor angels, nor rulers, nor things present, nor things to come,

Images: A collage of portraits of confirmed victims of the attacks.

nor powers, nor height, nor depth, nor anything else in all creation,

Image: A photograph of vehicles at ground zero covered in ash.

will be able to separate us from the love of God. (Rom. 8:35, 37–39)

Image: A photograph of two elderly people holding hands.

Cleanse us from all unrighteousness. (1 Jn. 1:9)

Image: A single photograph of a blue minivan with the words "Military Force! War!" painted on the windows.

For my thoughts are not your thoughts,
nor are your ways my ways, says the LORD. (Isa. 55:8)

Image: A single photograph of a green tow truck with the word "Revenge!" painted on the front bumper.

I therefore...beg you to lead a life worthy of the calling
to which you have been called, with all humility and gentleness,

> *Image*: A single photograph of a small crowd of teenagers holding a candlelight vigil at ground zero.

with patience, bearing with one another in love,

> *Image*: A photograph of a black female and a white male, holding each other.

making every effort to maintain the unity of the Spirit in the bond of peace.

> *Image*: A photograph of a man of Arab descent holding a single candle.

There is one body and one Spirit...
one Lord, one faith, one baptism, one God and Father of all,
who is above all and through all and in all. (Eph. 4:1–6)

> *Image*: A photograph of Buddhist monks at prayer.

Let love be genuine;
hate what is evil, hold fast to what is good;
love one another with mutual affection;
outdo one another in showing honor...

> *Image*: A photograph of Israeli men donating blood.

Rejoice in hope, be patient in suffering, persevere in prayer...

> *Image*: A photograph of men and women bowing their heads in a church sanctuary.

Rejoice with those who rejoice, weep with those who weep.
Live in harmony with one another...

> *Image*: photograph of Muslim men prostrated in prayer.

Do not repay anyone evil for evil...
live peaceably with all.
Beloved, never avenge yourselves,
but leave room for the wrath of God...
Do not be overcome by evil, but overcome evil with good. (Rom. 12:9–21)

> *Image*: A photograph of Afghani woman in prayer.

Final three images:

Incite Hope,
Not Hate...

Incite Hope,
Not Despair...

Incite Hope,
Rebuild the Ruins

Come What May

Habakkuk 1:1–4; 2:1–4

Then the LORD answered me and said: Write the vision; make it plain on tablets, so that a runner may read it. For there is still a vision for the appointed time; it speaks of the end, and does not lie. If it seems to tarry, wait for it; it will surely come, it will not delay. (Habakkuk 2:2–3)

We don't know much about the prophet named Habakkuk. He didn't get a lot of press like some of the other major prophets. His message was buried so far back in the Bible that it looks more like a last-minute footnote than a holy word from God. Most people can't remember how to spell the poor man's name, let alone pronounce it properly. And few readers have ever given much thought to reading the three short chapters the old prophet labored to put down on paper.

All in all, Habakkuk is a biblical nobody. We don't know where he came from. We don't know where he went. We don't know if his congregation slept through his sermons or took them to heart. We don't know much about this prophet Habakkuk. But we do know this: The prophet Habakkuk had holy nerve.

To stand before God, shake your fist, and shout out, "How long, O Lord, must I call out for help, and you will not listen?" Give it a try. See if you can do that; see if you can cry out, over and over again, night after night, year after year, for a world that has been *promised* by God but not yet delivered. See if you can do that without giving up and giving in and getting on with a life *without* God.

Everyone else in Habakkuk's world had tried to do that but failed. They started off with good and righteous intentions. The priests of Judah once worshiped and prayed as if their lives and the lives of their people depended on it, but not anymore. They saw too much of the world the way it really is, and they lost hope, lost their nerve. Now they spend their days at the country club and their evenings at the City Council and Lions Club meetings whenever they need a paltry invocation. The politicians of Jerusalem were once committed to advocating for the oppressed, the widow, the orphans, the poor; but they've seen too much of the world the way it is, and they feel powerless to change it. Word has it that they've sold out to Big Tobacco and the free vacation kickbacks at Pebble Beach. Even the people of Judah stopped coming to church; grew tired of hoping for a world that never came; forgot how to pray, how to believe, how to love something other than themselves, other than their stuff. You look long and hard enough at the world the way it is, with all its injustices and evils and struggles, and it's easy to feel overwhelmed and powerless.

But Habakkuk had this vision from God, and he wasn't about to let God, or his people, off the hook. Habakkuk had guts, nerve, mettle. He wasn't afraid to wrestle with God. He wasn't afraid to demand justice, to ask God why the world is the way it is, to ask God why the world isn't the way God intended it to be.

I've heard a lot of those questions over the last two weeks, in the wake of September 11. *Why?* Why did such profound, extreme evil visit our land and annihilate our brothers and sisters? Why is the world the way it is? Why *does* the rain fall on the just and the unjust? Where is justice? How long, O Lord, will we call out for justice, and not be heard?

Habakkuk gets his answer from God, and it is our answer, too.

When the things you work for become the things that I, since the beginning of creation, have longed for, says the Lord; when your way of life intersects with my vision for your life; when you have desired with sufficient strength the righteousness that the world says is impossible; on that day, my kingdom will come, and my will in all its fullness will be done.

But in the meantime, says God, hold on, keep watch. And we live in the meantime, don't we? The time between the world as it is and the world as it shall be. It is our time, the time God has given you and me to sanctify, to make holy. The vision of God has already been worked out, but the maps have not entirely been drawn. The vision of the world as it should be has already been divinely imagined; but it is up to us to trust sufficiently in that vision and dare, with God's grace, to draw the maps. How will we get there?

It begins with telling the truth about our world and about our ourselves. It begins with standing before God in sackcloth and ashes and confessing our complicity in the shortsighted, self-absorbed, self-serving ways of this world. That's why Habakkuk can be so daring before God. Habakkuk is honest. Habakkuk genuinely longs for the world that God has promised and is unafraid to confess that it's not the world his people have desired with sufficient strength.

I have to ask myself, ask all of you, if that is true of us. Are the things we've been working for in the world the very things God longs to give us? Before September 11, 2001, what were we working for? What was our heart's desire? In Habakkuk's day, people cried out, "Peace, peace," when there was no peace. I have heard it said in recent days, "The world will never be the same again," but an honest posture before God reveals that the world was broken long before September 11.

Four weeks ago a twenty-six-year-old woman stood at the edge of a Seattle bridge, contemplating the decision to end her life with a jump; she didn't do so in *peace.* Hundreds of motorists, after hours of waiting, began to taunt the woman. One officer reported that motorists were shouting, "Jump, bitch, jump." Other onlookers cursed the woman, who was distraught over a relationship. She had delayed their daily commute to the world's largest software company.

The officers first on the scene reported that motorists passing in the opposite direction stopped and added to the chorus of taunts. They succeeded. Though the mediation team tried desperately to stop the jumper, the woman ended the four-hour standoff by leaping from the bridge. She miraculously survived the jump with a spinal fracture and chest and abdominal injuries and is expected to recover.

The world will never be the same again, we say. Like Habakkuk, we should hope not. When we are honest about it, we cannot hope for a return to such a world. Like the people of Habakkuk's day, we've grown so weary of the world as it is that we've called it good and washed our hands of it. There is a lot of good in this world; but there is a lot of brokenness, a lot of injustice, a lot of sin we call good that isn't. Habakkuk, the sentinel, stands in our midst today and announces that a new world is coming: something so pure and so true that only those who tell the truth can see it, something so enduring only those who endure in righteousness will inherit it.

When you face the world honestly, when you see it in all its brokenness and dare to confess that it's not all so good, the greatest obstacle to that righteous life is discouragement, and discouragement slowly erodes into apathy. There has been a tremendous outpouring of love and volunteerism over the last two weeks. People doing extraordinary things: giving money, donating blood, lighting candles, praying. I fear, however, that it will be short-lived, that we will return to business as usual, that we will climb down from Habakkuk's watchtower and surrender our distinctive Christian vocation to the diluted, self-accommodating cause of philanthropy. Habakkuk doesn't preach an ethic of random, casual volunteerism. Habakkuk has sold out to a God who demands far more than the leftovers we so freely call *sacrifice.*

That is where the church distinguishes itself from the rest of the world. Compassion, justice, and the stewardship of our lives are not options or accessories to the Christian life. These are what we do; they are a critical part of our spiritual DNA, in the job description. We sell out to a lifetime vocation, and we receive our strength to go on doing it not because we are rewarded by the world for our efforts, but because we possess a larger vision of the way things should be according to God, and we trust in the truth of that vision more than the sober facts of life.

Come what may, says Habakkuk, I will without fail stand at the watchtower and announce that the day of the Lord's justice is on the horizon, almost here. If it seems to tarry, I will wait for it. It will surely come.

> Though the fig tree does not blossom, and no fruit is on the vines; though the produce of the olive fails and the fields yield no food; though the flock is cut off from the fold and there is no herd in the stalls, yet I will rejoice in the LORD; I will exult in the God of my salvation. GOD, the Lord, is my strength; he makes my feet like the feet of a deer, and makes me tread upon the heights. (Hab. 3:17–19)

We are all of us Habakkuk. We have all been called to be messengers in this world. God tells Habakkuk, "Write down the message on a stone tablet. Make it simple, easy to read, like a billboard that can be read from the highway. Do not make it complex; keep it simple. Write it down on a stone; write what you see coming into the world."

Each of you received a stone, a Mexican beach pebble, when you entered worship today. I want you to take those stones you have this morning, and using a permanent marker that the ushers will pass around, write down the message. Spend some quiet time reflecting on your life, reflecting on the *word* that God has put on your heart in the aftermath of the September 11 tragedy, the word that God has put on your heart to share with the world. It's not just a word, it's a mission—your mission. It is what you will do. It is the one tangible thing you will do, not just this week, but the one mission you will fulfill from here on out that will point to the coming of God's kingdom in this world. Forgiveness. Peace. Hope. Faith. Tolerance. Justice. What's the word God has given you? God has given it to you; God will give it to you again, if you ask for it. And when He gives it to you, it is your mission to go speak it, preach it, live it out.

Write it down on this stone. One word. And after you've written it down, bring it up to the altar; place it before the altar, as a sign of your offering, your sacrifice, your commitment. This week, a few of our members will gather up these stones and hike into the creek beds that surround this city; they will scatter these stones for the world to see. Imagine that. A mountain biker gets a flat tire out at Trabuco Creek trail, and as he bends over to repair the tube, he sees a stone lying there, bearing the word *Love* or *Faith* or *Mercy.* Maybe, in that moment of grace, he will get it. A runner stops in her tracks to tie her shoes, and as she completes the double knot, she catches sight of a stone bearing the message *Patience* or *Forgiveness* or *Repentance.* Perhaps it will be the very word she needed most to hear in that moment.

Write it down on stones, says the Lord to Habakkuk. Keep it simple. Make it plain, so that people passing by will see it and believe.

ART GALLERY

Major Motion Picture Clips

Based on actual events in 1838, *Amistad* (1997) is the story of captured African slaves who took over their transport ship in a bloody revolt with the hopes of returning to their homeland. After the slaves are caught and imprisoned, their leader, Cinque (Djimon Hounsou), unable to understand the language or court system of America, tries to communicate his desire to return home to his defense lawyer, Roger Baldwin (Matthew McConaughey), and former slave Theodore Joadson (Morgan Freeman). The men plead for help with their groundbreaking court case from former president John Quincy Adams (Anthony Hopkins).

I suggest a very powerful scene, near the end of the film, that depicts the captured slaves awaiting the verdict of their case. While waiting, one of the slaves reads from a picture-book Bible and engages Yambain in a conversation regarding the plight of Jesus Christ, who, like the slaves, was captured and tried unjustly for a crime he didn't commit. Introduced to numerous images of the cross, Yamba comes to understand its redemptive power and the fearlessness with which Jesus faced the unknown. The scene concludes as the slaves are ushered out to the roadside and led back to the courtroom for the verdict. Along the way, they see the masts of three ships in the harbor—a remarkable resemblance to the three crosses at Golgotha—and make the connection between their own story and the story of Jesus Christ.

Simple words and symbols of our faith can change the way others see the world and their own circumstances. It is the task of every Christian to present the liberating, transforming gospel in our own time and place. *(VHS, 1:35:15–1:40:51) Total time: 5:46.*

"Man on the Street"

Interview people on the street, or people in your congregation, inviting responses to the following question:

If you could do one thing to make the world a better place, what would it be?

Edit these responses and present them at the conclusion of the sermon as an invitation to imagine the kind of world to which Habakkuk pointed.

Pop Music

U2, "Peace on Earth"

This song expresses our generation's frustration over the endless violence in the world and the disparity between the world as it is and the world promised by God. Written by Bono on the day of the Omagh bombing in Ireland (August 15, 1998) in which twenty-nine people were killed and dozens severely injured, the song expresses an honest struggle to believe in an age in which "hope and history won't rhyme" and the song of peace gets stuck in the throat. While we wait for "heaven on earth," will we become the very "monster" we "mock," or will Jesus throw us a line?

Invite a soloist to perform the song during the dedication of stones at the conclusion of the sermon.

Images

Graffiti, stones, people at prayer, billboard advertisements.

Mission

As noted in the sermon, Mexican beach pebbles were given to the worshipers as they entered the sanctuary. Any small, smooth stone will serve this purpose. At the appropriate time in the worship experience, invite the ushers to distribute permanent markers for the worshipers to use for the closing dedication exercise. During this reflective time in the service, project various words on the screen to inspire the congregation and lead them to a personal response.

The Sound of Sheer Silence

1 Kings 19:1–19

Now there was a great wind, so strong that it was splitting mountains and breaking rocks in pieces before the LORD, but the LORD was not in the wind; and after the wind an earthquake, but the LORD was not in the earthquake; and after the earthquake a fire, but the LORD was not in the fire; and after the fire a sound of sheer silence. (1 Kings 19:11b–12)

So you get to that point in your life where you've got to make a hard decision about something terribly important to you, or you've reached the end of the rope in your life and you're hanging on by mere threads, or a crisis broadsides you out of nowhere and it appears as though you're out of options. Maybe it's the job that's heading nowhere, or a new job that promises to take you somewhere; maybe it's an illness, or a separation, or an empty bank account, or a wayward child.

Whatever it is, you get to that point where you need some help because it's something you either can't do alone or are afraid to do alone. So when the time is right, and the words finally come to you, you sit down in an empty room, or on a quiet hilltop, or in the sublime solitude of your BMW, and you say something like, "Okay, God, I'm here. I'm listening. I'm looking. I'm waiting. Show me a sign." And then you wait.

You've heard that this kind of thing works for religious people, right? Moses had a burning bush. Noah had a rainbow. The disciples had loaves and fishes. Paul had a bolt of lightning and the temporary blindness issue. Old Zechariah went mute. You'll take any one of those right now, right? Anything that will give you hope and reason to believe. Show me a sign, you say. Speak up. I'm all ears.

I've been there, just like you've been there, I know. When I was called by the bishop to pastor this church six years ago, I was there, wondering what God was up to in sending me to a start-up church with no money, no building, and few people—show me a sign. I was there when my forty-eight-year-old father battled cancer and we strained desperately to keep the door locked to death's dark visitor—show me a sign. I was there when my two-year-old son was hooked to a respirator with a brain injury and his fragile life was hanging in the balance—show me a sign. We've all been there.

Frederick Buechner writes about being there many years ago. His anorexic daughter was dying, her body slowly wasting away. She refused treatment. And the doctors told him that she would die without serious intervention. But Buechner, after so many failed attempts to break through to her, was powerless to change the situation. He writes,

> I remember sitting parked by the roadside once, terribly depressed and afraid about my daughter's illness and what was going on in our family, when out of nowhere a car came along down the highway with a license plate that bore on it the one word out of all the words in the dictionary that I needed most to see exactly then. The word was TRUST. What do you call a moment like that? Something to laugh off as the kind of joke life plays on us every once in a while? The Word of God? I am willing to believe that maybe it was something of both, but for me it was an epiphany. The owner of the car turned out to be, as I suspected, a trust officer in a bank, and not long ago, having read an account I wrote of the incident somewhere, he found out where I lived and one afternoon brought me the license plate itself, which sits propped up on a bookshelf in my house to this day. It is rusty around the edges and a little battered, and it is also as holy a relic as I have ever seen.[1]

Maybe God has a sense of humor, or maybe this is the way God so often chooses to talk to us. It's not the kind of communication we've come to expect from God. We look for the big stuff, the seemingly impossible stuff, like burning bushes and miraculous healings and thunderous voices and neon lights. Instead, we most often get the painful, awful silence from God. It's not our preferred method of divine communication; but in it there is, when we have ears to hear, considerable grace.

I want you to look carefully at the way God chooses to deal with Elijah, because it does not require a stretch of the imagination to see ourselves in his story. Elijah is locked deep in a cave in the highlands of Israel. He's having one of those Maalox moments in his life; the queen wants him dead for going postal on her cronies. Elijah is a prophet; and more than that, he is to the world of the prophets what Elvis Presley was to the world of rock and roll. He is the king of prophecy, with a king-sized mission. His nation has sold out; his people are worshiping clay gods. Ever since King David breathed his last a hundred years before, things haven't been the same. People don't know God anymore; faith has eroded into agnostic, benign superstition. Israel is dying a slow, terrible death, and Elijah is the last remnant of the way things used to be.

So he finally snaps one day. Makes *Gladiator* look like a bike ride with E.T. He kills four hundred prophets of the clay gods in a heartbeat, right in front of old King Ahab. So Ahab runs home with his tail between his legs, reports the news to his dreaded wife, Jezebel, and everybody knows you don't mess with Jezebel. Elijah did. Jezebel rages. And the king of prophecy runs for cover with a bull's-eye on his back and a bounty on his head.

So here he sits, deep in the protective womb of a dark cave. He wants to die; more than Jezebel wants him dead, Elijah wants to die. He knows the headhunters are already on the way. He knows that he's won the battle but he's lost the war; he's toasted and buttered, done. So he's despairing; hopeless; thinking seriously about giving the Dr. Kevorkian hotline a try because he doesn't want to live, because the way he sees it, there's nothing left to live for. Elijah has failed at his mission; his mission was his life. He hides in the darkness, his tomb, and waits to die.

But God is in the business of giving people like Elijah a sign. The plot, the pacing, the promise of the text cries out for a sign, right? So we look for it, wait for it. And it comes, but not as we expected.

"Now there was a great wind," goes the story, "so strong that it was splitting mountains and breaking rocks in pieces before the LORD." And we say to ourselves, there it is, there's the sign. "But," says the story, "the LORD was not in the wind." Then "after the wind [there was a great] earthquake," goes the story, and again we think this must be it. "But the LORD was not in the earthquake." And suddenly things aren't looking too good for old Elijah. "And after the earthquake a fire," and we say all right, there it is, at last, "But the LORD was not in the fire," goes the story, and like Elijah we wonder if the Lord is anywhere in the story. But "after the fire," says the story, "a sound of sheer silence." Nothing. Nada. It's as if time had just stopped, as if the world had just shut down and all of life just held its breath, even God. Silence. Nothing.

It's bad enough when our spouses give us the silent treatment; when God gives it, it's almost more than we can take. Silence. We don't do well with silence. We assume that when God is silent, God is absent. So we go where the noise is. We play music in elevators and shopping malls to fill the silence; we fill in the gaps of our conversation with aimless chatter just to avoid silence. We'll leave a TV or radio on in the other room just to avoid the staggering silence of our lives. We wrap noise around us like a blanket just to insulate us from the sound of sheer silence.

Rabbi Lawrence Kushner wrote a book called *God Was in This Place and I, I Did Not Know.* In it he makes reference to Solomon's temple, God's original dwelling place on earth. First Kings says that the room was empty except for a single throne, which was also empty. On either side were two gold cherubim spreading their wings over it. The room was completely silent, undisturbed, save for one day out of the year, the Day of Atonement, when the high priest came in to make amends for the people. He had a single purpose for his visit to the temple room: to utter the holy name of God, which posed a bit of a problem because no one quite knew how to pronounce the name of God; the name of God was written in all vowels. No one dared even try to pronounce the name, nor were they permitted to. As the high priest inhaled and exhaled, he could begin to hear the sound of God's name—*Yah-weh*—on his lips. God's holy name, uttered with each breath, could be heard and spoken only in the silence of that sacred place. And just in case the high priest got the name wrong and was struck dead by God, the other priests would tie a rope around his leg so that they could pull him out without risking their own lives.[2]

For Elijah, something's not right. It's too quiet, spooky, like a Stephen King novel. Nothing but the sound of sheer silence outside the cave. The silence, however, is the sign.

He could handle the whistle of the winds and the rumble of the earth and the crackling of the fire, but the sound of sheer silence has put a lump in his throat and sent his heart racing. He raises his wizened frame, wraps his face in his coat to keep from seeing whatever it is he might run into out there, and stumbles to the entrance to the cave to greet the silence. And standing there, God finally speaks. "Elijah, what are you doing in there?" And as if God didn't already know, Elijah tells the story: "Your people have sold out; your altars have been destroyed; nobody gives a damn about you anymore. So I got a little carried away, wiped out Jezebel's secret service, and now I'm a dead man. It's over, Lord. I'm the last of your righteous remnant. There's no one left but me. It's all over. I don't have a prayer." "Elijah," says the Lord, "the story's not over; it's just beginning. Get up, stop wasting time, and get back to work. I'll cover your back on this one."

Why are we so afraid of the silence these days? Could it be that the noise we work so hard to create in our lives, and the noise with which we surround ourselves, actually conceals what lies within us—the needs, the pains, the passions, and the joys? Could it be that the silence we try so hard to avoid is actually the doorway into discovering who we are and whose we are and how we are and why we are? Noise is concealing; silence is revealing. And it just might be that the only sure way of hearing God is in the silence, where you've got to literally strain to hear what he might be saying. And it very well may be the only sure way of hearing what those around us are saying. What is spoken in the gaps, in the silence, in the unspoken moments of our lives might hold more truth than any spoken words could possibly bear.

Southern Californians have had more than their share of tragedies in the previous decade. Like Elijah, we've seen the fires, the earthquakes, the winds and the floods, and more bloodshed than we'd have cared to witness in an entire lifetime. Just after the ground shook under Northridge, the NBC news network aired a weeklong series on whether or not God was trying to tell us something through this series of tragic events—"acts of God," as we've come to call them. They interviewed pastors and priests and rabbis and theologians on the matter, each of whom concluded that God was using these events to convince us to get our act together; these are all warnings, they said over and over again, God's notice that if we don't straighten up pretty soon, we'll be next. Not one of them dared to say simply that they didn't know if God had anything at all to do with these events. Not one of them dared to say nothing at all, for fear, perhaps, that no one would listen to their silence.

We embarrass God with all that noise and senseless chatter; we sound more like a noisy gong and a clanging symbol than anything remotely resembling the people of God. When Jesus calms the storm for his disciples, who are frantic with senseless prattle, what does he say? "Shut up!" I've often wondered if it was the storm or the disciples he was commanding; both were silenced.

I want to air my own weeklong series for the evening news. I don't want to interview pastors or theologians; we enjoy too much the sound of our own voices. Instead, I want to interview Sunday school teachers and Little League coaches and accountants and custodians; I want to ask them if they think God is trying to tell us something when they see the sun first kiss the sky in the silent dawn of a new day, or when they peek over their child's bed in the quiet darkness of the night and watch in all the wonder and hush of that moment, or when the power goes out and the TV shuts off and the phone can no longer ring and the clock stops ticking and there's nothing to do but sit in stillness and think, or when the rattle in the car for some mysterious reason just doesn't rattle anymore. I don't know what they'd say, but I know what Elijah would say. Get ready, because the Lord, the God of hosts, is about to say something really big if you can bear the silence long enough to hear it.

There is a very moving scene in the movie *Shawshank Redemption* in which the main character, Andrew Dufresne, who is serving a life sentence for a crime he didn't commit, locks himself inside the guard's room and plays Mozart's *The Marriage of Figaro* over the PA system for the entire prison to hear. He was given two weeks in solitary confinement for that daring act. On his first day out of the hole, he is talking to his friends in the mess hall. "Was it worth it," one of them asks? "Piece of cake," he says, "easiest time I ever did." "One week in the hole is like a year," somebody says. Andrew replies, "I had Mr. Mozart down there with me." "You mean they let you tote that record player down there with you." "No," he replies, "I had it in here," as he points to his head, "and in here," as he taps his heart. "That's the beauty of it. They can't take that from you. You need it down there so you don't forget...that there are places in this world that aren't made out of stone, that there's something inside that they can't get to, that they can't touch, that's yours." "What are you talking about?" asks Red. "Hope. Hope."

It is out of the silence that God's word is revealed and God's hope is born and it is into the silence that we are called to return, away from the noise, in the gaps, where we strain to hear the music that God plays deep within us, the music that sends us forward, the sign in which a new mission is revealed, in an unstilled world.

ART GALLERY

Major Motion Picture Clips

Clip 1: *Shawshank Redemption* (1994). Use as noted in the sermon. *(VHS, 1:07:00–1:12:45) Total time: 5:45.*

Clip 2: In *Falling Down* (1993), a laid-off defense worker, Bill Foster (Michael Douglas), who is kept from seeing his child on her birthday by a restraining order, looks at the landscape of moral decay in Los Angeles on one hot, congested day and, after being mugged, finally snaps. What follows is his bitter and pathetic mission of justice, vengeance, and vindication.

This scene, the opening cut for the movie, introduces Bill Foster, stuck in a major traffic jam on an L.A. freeway on a hot afternoon. As the stress and noise of the moment overwhelms him, Foster simply steps out of his car and walks off the freeway. *(VHS, 0:02:22–0:04:54) Total time: 2:32.*

Pop Music

Collective Soul, "Listen"

A song that could very well be Elijah's theme song, about a character walking alone in the desert, lost in the "isolation of his soul," whose "prophecies have failed," who's clothing himself "in shields of despair" while the speaking silence longs to be heard, if only his "heart could open up and listen."

Bobby McFerrin, "Common Threads"

A moving, lulling voice-instrumental that gently soars and slowly fades. Theme song from the movie, *Common Threads: Stories from the Quilt* (1990).

Creed, "Faceless Man"

Spending a day alone by the river, where it's quiet and the

wind stands still, a man discovers that it's funny how silence speaks sometimes when you're alone. Looking into the water he sees the reflection of a faceless man, whose yoke is easy and whose burden is light, and desires to choose to live for always.

Poetry

T. S. Eliot, "Ash Wednesday"

If the lost word is lost, if the spent word is spent
If the unheard, unspoken
Word is unspoken, unheard;
Still is the unspoken word, the Word unheard,
The Word without a word, the Word within
The world and for the world;
And the light shone in the darkness and
Against the Word the unstilled world still whirled
About the centre of the silent Word.

O my people, what have I done unto thee.

Where shall the word be found, where will the word
Resound? Not here, there is not enough silence.[3]

Images

Windblown trees, earthquake rubble, firestorms, a hand over the mouth.

Daily Bread

Matthew 6:7–13

"Give us this day our daily bread." (Matthew 6:11)

You are about to become a refugee. You have just ten minutes to prepare for a journey into an unknown future. You know only one thing for sure: You will never return home. Buses and trucks are already on the way to take you, your family, and your neighbors to the nearest harbor where, if you are one of the lucky ones, you'll board a boat and sail to a safe, foreign land.

The task now before you is to pack a single bag for the journey. Into the bag you can pack only three items, the total weight of which you must be able to carry by yourself, which means, of course, that you'll have to leave the baby grand piano behind, among a few other things.

So the clock is ticking. Ten minutes. Three items. One bag. What will it be?

Is it a tough choice for you? Of all the things we own, all the stuff that fills our closets and garages and dressers and cupboards, we all have a few things we simply cannot imagine going without. And if we're at all honest with ourselves, we'll confess that we all have too many things we can live without, even if we cannot imagine doing so.

It's called affluenza—the drive to acquire and consume and accumulate more than we need and more than what's good for us to get. It's a disease that is so widespread in our culture, so prevalent and insidious in each of our lives, that it's hard to even diagnose on our own. We often do not even know we suffer from it, and Madison Avenue works overtime to keep it that way.

It's believed that you and I, on average, see or hear as many as ten thousand advertisements a day—from the labels on the clothes we wear to the bumper stickers on backs of our cars; from radio, television, newspapers, and billboards to logos, slogans, jingles, and trademark sounds. We are constantly reminded that there's something missing in our lives, that there's one more thing we must have that we cannot possibly live without. Buy Pepsi. Get Stuff. And we do. Our closets are jammed with stuff, but the irony of our consumptive appetite is that we often long for salt to satisfy our deepest thirst, and it is never enough.

So Jesus gives us the prescription, in the form of a prayer. "Give us this day our daily bread." Which is really nothing more than asking for the very basics. That's all we have a right to ask God for—just the basics, something as simple as bread, and simply enough bread for today. That is all. But the prayer is a promise that daily bread is enough.

This prayer is grounded in Old Testament history, in the Exodus story. Go back to the Exodus story, and you'll recall the great deliverance from the slavery of Egypt. The Hebrew refugees hightail it through the Red Sea and come out the other side in one piece and free at last. It's looking like a new day for God's people, a fresh start, a clean break. And now they figure they're going to get a taste of what it's like to live on the other side, right?

But no sooner do they step foot on dry land than some hungry soul sidles up to Moses and says, "Excuse me, Moses. Just one quick question—who packed the Captain Crunch?" And Moses says, "You know, funny you should ask..."

They've come all this way, right? They've overcome impossible odds. But now they're faced with the most basic of issues out there in the desert—hunger. That's when their relationship with God is truly tested. Is this God who leads us out of slavery going to leave us out here in the desert to starve?

So God performs another miracle. Each morning, while the dew is still wet on the tents, God causes bread to come down from heaven. It's not great stuff, mind you. It's called manna, and it's a far cry from even the bread of slavery that Pharaoh fed them. But it's a start. And God says to them, "I'm going to give you just enough manna every day to keep you going. Gather only what you need. Don't hoard it; don't save it for another day. I didn't lead you out here to eat; I led you out here to get to know me, to listen to me, to learn from me. I'm going to give you daily bread, and you're going to learn to trust that what I give you is all you'll really need."

We would do well to learn, as the Hebrews did, the meaning of enough. Jesus tells us that our Father in heaven knows what we need, and in seeking his kingdom first, all the rest will be given to us. Which is another way of saying that the faithful have everything they need, and that is a strange thing to affirm in a culture that is held captive by the tyranny of scarcity, this fear of not having enough, this drive to consume and acquire and stockpile and accumulate.

If we were to get out of bed tomorrow and say to ourselves, "I have everything I need," would our lives be any different? Christians start the day by shaving it. They cut out what will be too much. They practice what Thoreau called "driving life into a corner and reducing it to its lowest terms."

Christians have a model for this kind of stewardship. Paul writes to the Philippians and says, "I have learned to be content with whatever I have. I know what it is to have little, and I know what it is to have plenty. In any and all circumstances I have learned the secret of being well-fed and of going hungry, of having plenty and of being in need" (Phil. 4:11b–12).

I want to experience that same freedom, but I know it's going to take some work; it's a different world from Paul's. I struggle with wanting more than I need; acquiring what I do not need, I find I want even more; and failing to get what I cannot have, I too often envy those who can.

Two billion credit card solicitations are mailed out each year to people like you and me. The average American carries a credit card debt of $25,000, or about $4,000 for every man, woman, and child in North America. It's the price we pay for Mastercard's so-called "priceless" moments of life. The "power to get," as Visa calls it, has got us.[1]

The plastic we carry in our wallets is often the enemy of contentment. When my family made the commitment last year to making cash-only purchases, with the exceptions of our mortgage and car payments, we discovered a little of what Paul meant when he spoke of being content with what one has in life. No more credit card purchases, no more monthly balances, no more minimum payments. What we cannot buy with cash, we do not need. Pharaoh lost his grip. His chains no longer rattle.

We've also made a commitment to what many have called "Buy-Nothing Days." One day a week we have committed ourselves to buying nothing. One day a week we fast from buying, removing ourselves from a system that wants us to believe that consumption leads to contentment. At least one day a week we pass the coffeehouse without stopping in for a café mocha and we drive by the gas station without topping off the tank. Paul's confession of faith becomes our own. One day out of the week, we affirm that we have everything we need.

John Francis Kavanaugh suggests,

> If you are relatively happy with your life, if you enjoy spending time with your children, playing with them and talking with them; if you like nature, if you enjoy sitting in your yard or on your front steps, if your sexual life is relatively happy; if you have a peaceful sense of who you are and are stabilized in your relationships, if you like to pray in solitude, if you just like talking to people, visiting them, spending time in conversation with them, if you enjoy living simply, if you sense no need to compete with your friends or neighbors—*what good are you economically* in terms of our system? You haven't spent a nickel yet.
>
> However, if you are unhappy and distressed, if you are living in anxiety and confusion, if you are unsure of yourself and your relationships, if you find no happiness in your family or sex life, if you can't bear being alone or living simply—you will crave much. You will want more.[2]

And so we pray, "Give us this day our daily bread." Then we stand with Paul and affirm the contentment that comes from having everything we need. Manna falls from heaven, and we are filled with the things from above.

But the prayer cuts even deeper. It is one of the most honest, daring petitions of the Lord's Prayer. It forces us to be honest about ourselves, about our lifestyles, about the infinite number of ways our conspicuous consumption leaves mere crumbs for others to gather up from beneath our tables. It is as much a confession as it is a petition. It calls to our attention that the tennis shoes we wear have been stitched by children in some distant Third World land—a land with a GNP far less than the net worth of the professional athletes who endorse those shoes. It calls us to think twice about the plight of those who maintain our lawns and gardens and clean our homes, those who work the strawberry fields and bus our tables for a less-than-living wage. "The spoil of the poor is in your houses," says the prophet Isaiah (3:14). We cannot escape his indictment without committing ourselves to remembering and caring for the poor among us.

I know of a family who takes this seriously. The parents are tithers; so are their children. Each month this family drives to the local market, where the children spend 10 percent of their monthly allowance on food and clothing, which they then transport to the local shelter for distribution to women and children in poverty. From creed to deed this family affirms that none of us are fed until all of us are fed. The daily bread for which they pray is blessed, broken, and given as bread for the world.

Think twice before uttering this prayer. Strap yourselves in, put on your crash helmet—you are putting yourself in God's redemptive path of justice in which the scales are balanced, and all to which you cling may be shaken loose as your prayer rises to heaven. Those to whom much is given, much is required.

Thomas Lynch, poet and mortician, tells the story about leaving a cemetery one day with a local priest,

> a man who loved golf and gold ciboria and vestments made of Irish linen; a man who drove a great black sedan with wine-red interior and who always had his eye on the cardinal's job—this same fellow...felt called upon to instruct me thus: "No bronze coffin for me. No Sir! No orchids or roses or limousines. The plain pine box is the one I want, a quiet Low Mass and the pauper's grave. No pomp and circumstance."
>
> He wanted, he explained, to be an example of simplicity, of prudence, of piety and austerity—all priestly and, apparently, Christian virtues. When I told him that he needn't wait, that he could begin his ministry of good example even today, that he could quit the country club and do his hacking at the public links and trade his brougham for a used Chevette; that free of his Florsheims and cashmeres and prime ribs, free of his bingo nights and building funds, he could become, for Christ's sake, the very incarnation of Francis himself, or Anthony of Padua; when I said, in fact, that I would be willing to assist him in this, that I would gladly distribute his savings and credit cards among the worthy poor of the parish, and that I would, when the sad duty called, bury him for free in the manner he would have, by then, become accustomed to; when I told your man these things, he said nothing at all, but turned his wild eye on me...

> What I was trying to tell the fellow was, of course, that being a dead saint is no more worthwhile than being a dead philodendron or a dead angelfish. Living is the rub, and always has been. Living saints still feel the stigmata of this vale of tears, the ache of chastity and the pangs of conscience.[3]

"Give us this day our daily bread," we pray. And he does. He takes bread, blesses and breaks it, and says, "Remember." Then we gather around his table and pray the words of the great thanksgiving: "Make this bread be for us the body of Christ, that we may be for the world the body of Christ, redeemed by his blood."

It is. We are. And yes, it is enough.

ART GALLERY

Major Motion Picture Clips

In the movie *The Money Pit* (1986), Shelley Long and Tom Hanks buy the house of their dreams, only to watch it fall apart the moment they move in. In this light-hearted, comical scene, Hanks discovers that his newly purchased dream home is not what he bargained for. *(VHS 0:38:32–0:1:26) Total time: 2:56.*

"Man on the Street"

With video camera and microphone, interview members of your congregation on the following question:

If you were about to become a refugee and could only pack three items (your Bible is a freebie), what would you pack?

The video team in my church interviewed eight members of the congregation for this component of the worship experience. Responses included: journals, a Sonic Air toothbrush, family photo albums, personal letters, a Swiss Army knife, matches, and so on.

Use this footage at the beginning of the sermon as you set up the introductory question.

Pop Music

Don Henley, "Gimme What You Got"
The present-day prophet and cultural critic mocks our consumptive appetite and reminds us that you don't see hearses with luggage racks.

Collective Soul, "Run"
Lamenting the consumptive contagion of our culture and a world of purchase, which eventually erodes into boredom, the wasting of time, and a processed sanity, this honest lyric expresses the deep spiritual hunger of our generation and the longing for a cure to the relentless pursuit of stuff.

Images

Refugees, poverty, soup kitchens and shelters, communion bread.

Mission

Establish short-term missions within your congregation, such as visits to local soup kitchens, food banks, and homeless shelters.

Introduce a small group study using Tony Campolo's *Affluenza* video resource, available by purchase or rental through your denomination's media center.

Life after God

Matthew 5:13–20

"You are the light of the world. A city built on a hill cannot be hid. No one after lighting a lamp puts it under the bushel basket, but on the lampstand, and it gives light to all in the house. In the same way, let your light shine before others, so that they may see your good works and give glory to your Father in heaven." (Matthew 5:14–16)

Well, I'll be looking for him again this year. He's there every year, right? The shirtless, red-wigged madman behind the goalpost, holding his John 3:16 sign high above his head during every field goal attempt. It wouldn't be a Super Bowl without that guy. He's become part of the game, part of the tradition, like the trillion dollar commercial spots and the less-than-spectacular, always overdone halftime shows. I look for him every year, that man, and for the lucky guy sitting behind him who paid $1,200 for his seat only to see the back of some big white sign. The messenger is there every year, or some variation of him, a visible sign of God's presence bobbing up and down in the vast ocean of human chaos.

In the chaos and frenzy of our lives, it wouldn't hurt to have our own little red-wigged madman following us along, raising up his bold white sign every time we looked his way, reminding us that God is here, even here, in the chaos that is our life. More and more of us are asking that question, you know—"*Where* is God in all of this?" Before the dawning of postmodernism, before time and space were measured in nanoseconds and kilobytes, back in the days when change was slow enough to chart and our lives had some degree of predictability, back then we were asking the "why" questions—"Why did God allow this to happen? Why am I in this mess? Why is the world the way it is?" Back then we figured that if we just knew the *why* of life, we could fix our problems, dig ourselves out of our mess. But it's a different world now. Things move much faster. Life is increasingly becoming more complex. It sometimes feels as though we're on one of those globes in our junior high geography class; and while the teacher isn't looking the class clown is just spinning that thing as fast as he can, and all we can do is hold on. The truth is that we do not have much time or energy anymore to ask the *why* questions, to dig ourselves out of our mess; it may be, too, that we are afraid of the answers. We are a generation that has discovered that answers, propositions, and proofs can neither save us nor satisfy our deep longing for the personal experience of spiritual community. We're not after answers; we're after God. We're not after religion; we're after a relationship. In the postmodern world, we mostly just want to know *where* to find God, where to find community in God, so we can stay grounded and connected while the world goes on spinning.

Jesus is preaching his Sermon on the Mount. He tells us there that those whom he calls blessed in this world are those who aspire to live out of God's strength rather than their own—the mourning, the meek, the merciful, the pure in heart, the *cheese makers*, to quote Monty Python. Which leads him into today's passage about the difference between those who love religion and those who love God, about salt that has lost its taste and lamps that have become dome lights for the insiders rather than lighthouses for the outsiders.

Jesus is talking about the people in the know, the people in power, those who have all the answers but apparently do not have the lives to match them. They are people not unlike us in many ways. They're hard-working, tithe-paying, creed-saying people who have a lot going for them, not the least of which is their complete loyalty to God's law. They know what God requires of them; they do their best to follow God's commandments; they cross their *t*'s and dot their *i*'s with such precision. The only problem, says Jesus, is that they seem more interested in themselves than they are with God. Religion has become for them a means of self-glorification, so that whatever light their lives are able to shine seems to shine only on themselves. Which is why Jesus says we are to have a righteousness that exceeds theirs, to let our light shine in such a way that it gives glory to God, not to us.

Fyodor Dostoyevsky's novel *The Brothers Karamazov* spoke of this condition in the church of his day. In the famous chapter "The

Grand Inquisitor," he tells the chilling story of the church's thirst for power and its fear of the radical, unpredictable presence of Jesus. Set in the days of the Spanish Inquisition, in Seville, Jesus has just returned to earth. He comes to Seville and walks toward the massive Gothic cathedral, healing the sick and the lame and blessing the people in the square. The people cry out, "Hosannah. It's Him. It's Him."

Meanwhile, a funeral procession slowly moves toward the cathedral steps, bearing the body of a seven-year-old girl, the only child of a noble citizen. Her casket, covered in flowers, is being carried to the cathedral. The people call to him, and he comes to them. The mother of the child, falling to her knees, cries out, "If it is You, then raise up my child!" He gazes with compassion, and his lips softly pronounce the words, *Talitha cumi*—"Damsel, I say unto thee, arise." And the child sits up and looks at the people around her, and smiles, with astonished, wide-open eyes.

But standing in the shadows of the cathedral is the Cardinal Grand Inquisitor, an old man of almost ninety, tall and straight, with a withered face and sunken eyes, who sees Jesus' arrival as a threat to his authority. The cardinal has Jesus arrested and placed in a solitary prison cell. Later that evening, the cardinal comes alone to visit his royal prisoner, asking Jesus, "Why have you come to get in our way? You have no right to add to what was said by you in former times. Why have you come to get in our way?" He threatens to have Jesus burned at the stake in the morning.

> When the Inquisitor falls silent, he waits for a certain amount of time to hear what his Captive will say in response. He finds His silence difficult to bear...The old man would like the Other to say something to him, even if it is bitter, terrible. But he suddenly draws near to the old man without saying anything and quietly kisses him on his bloodless, ninety-year-old lips. That is his only response. The old man shudders...goes to the open door, opens it and says to Him: "Go and do not come back...do not come back at all...ever...ever!" And he releases him into the town's dark streets and squares.[1]

Why do we come here to worship, Sunday after Sunday, fifty-two Sundays a year, for five, ten, thirty years—or a whole lifetime? Getting up early Sunday morning, getting ready, getting the children dressed, driving in all sorts of weather, sometimes not feeling too well ourselves, angry at the government, worried about our health and financial problems, dressed in our best and on our best behavior, walking into the building, greeting friends, singing hymns, praying prayers, reading scripture, listening to sermons, bringing our offering, taking the bread and cup...We call it the worship of God, but why do we do this?

I was in Dallas a couple of weeks ago on retreat with other young United Methodist pastors. Part of the program included spending a day with Bill Easum, a church consultant who, for several years now, has been a prophetic voice in the North American church. He's spent the second half of his life challenging churches to look critically at themselves, saying over and over again that if the church is going to survive and have anything relevant to say to the postmodern world, it's going to have to make some changes and give the church back to Jesus Christ. He has a wonderful way of shocking you with his comments; you might call him an ecclesiastical cattle prod. Speaking to a group of young ministers, Easum said, "The problem with the church today is that we're no longer churches, we're clubs. And we're no longer Christian, he said, but Unitarian, afraid to talk about the transforming power of Jesus and the distinctive nature of our Christian confession." It wasn't a slight on Unitarianism. It was simply a statement about our fear of speaking with particularity about our unique confession as Christians, our reluctance to get out of the way so that Jesus can have his way with us.

Why do we come here to worship week in and week out? Is it because we need religion, or is it because we need God? Jesus says there is a difference between the two, because you can be religious and still not enter the kingdom of God, but you can't have an authentic encounter with God without being forever changed because of it.

The truth about us is that we need God, not answers, not religion, not a club. And an even greater truth is that we need God now more than we ever have before, because that globe is spinning faster and faster and the gravity of God's grace is the only thing that keeps us from drifting off into space and getting lost forever.

Douglas Coupland's book *Life after God* offers a collection of stories about Generation X and its search for meaning in an age of despair and loneliness. One of the stories is about a young man in his twenties who has come to that point in his life where he sees himself as essentially broken inside; he seriously questions the road his life has taken and the compromises he has made over the years. He stops taking the pills that make his depression more bearable, and one morning, after pulling into the parking lot for work, he decides to turn around and drive several hours deep into a forest in northern British Columbia, looking for God. He pitches a tent in the rain-soaked forest, falls asleep, and the next morning, walks to a rushing stream, finds a small pool, and steps in the freezing water.

> I peel my clothes and step into the pool beside the burbling stream, onto polished rocks, and water so clear that it seems it might not even be really there...
>
> The water is so cold, this water that only yesterday was locked as ice up on the mountaintops. But the pain from the cold is a pain that does not matter to me. I strip my pants, my shirt, my tie, my underwear and they lie strewn on the gravel bar next to my blanket.
>
> And the water from the stream above me roars.
>
> Oh, does it roar! Like a voice that knows only one message, one truth—never-ending, like the clapping of hands and the cheers of the citizens upon the coronation of the king...cheering for hope and for that one voice that will speak to them.
>
> Now—here is my secret: I tell it to you with an openness of heart that I doubt I shall ever achieve again, so I pray that you are in a quiet room as you hear these words. My secret is that I need God—that I am sick and can no longer make it alone. I need God to help me give, because I no longer seem capable of giving; to help me be kind, as I no longer seem capable of kindness; to help me love, as I seem beyond being able to love.
>
> I walk deeper and deeper into the rushing water...The water enters my belly button and it freezes my chest, my arms, my neck. It reaches my mouth, my nose, my ears and the roar is so loud—this roar, this clapping of hands.
>
> These hands—the hands that heal; the hands that hold; the hands we desire because they are better than desire.
>
> I submerge myself in the pool completely. I grab my knees and I forget gravity and I float with the pool and yet, even here, I hear the roar of water, the roar of clapping hands.

> These hands—the hands that care, the hands that mold; the hands that touch the lips, the lips that speak the words—the words that tell us we are whole.[2]

You are the light of the world. You are the light of the world. You are the light of the world. That is who Jesus has made you to be. Write it down on a big white sign, put on your red wig, and shine.

ART GALLERY

Major Motion Picture Clips

Clip 1: *Notting Hill* (1999) tells the story of William (Hugh Grant), an unassuming bookstore owner in London's Notting Hill section, and Anna (Julia Roberts), a Hollywood actress, who, against the odds, are able to fall in love. After Anna wanders into William's shop while filming on location in London, the two share an instant attraction and find themselves attempting to forge a normal relationship despite Anna's stardom.

In this clip, William invites Anna to his sister's birthday party, where his entire family of down-to-earth, ordinary people are gathered together for a meal. At the dinner table, they initiate a contest for the last brownie, which will be awarded to the person at the table with the saddest, sorriest excuse for the way they are. After each family member offers his or her story, Anna offers up a moving, honest reflection on the perils of her rising star. *(VHS, 39:10–43:55) Total time: 4:45.*

Use this clip to illustrate themes of postmodern spirituality—community, vulnerability, relationships, and self-mocking—and to affirm that it's in this very context that our light shines in Christ.

Clip 2: *Good Will Hunting* (1997) tells the story of a South Boston whiz kid (Matt Damon) who elects to clean the halls of MIT rather than enter them to study, slacking his way through life as a janitor despite having all the intellectual tools of academic success. His natural ability to unravel complex equations attracts the attention of a professor who won't let him quit, a beautiful Harvard student who wants to save him, a sympathetic buddy who wants him to escape South Boston, and a counselor (Robin Williams) who encourages him and leads him to a dramatic transformation.

In this scene, Will's counselor, Sean, leads him to confront his painful past of having been abused by his father and helps Will to understand, "It's not your fault." This honest, tender scene contains explicit language that may be inappropriate for worship; be prepared to edit or mute the sound, if necessary. *(VHS, 1:46:50–1:50:30) Total time: 4:40.*

Clip 3: *X-Files: Fight the Future* (1998) finds Mulder and Scully in hot pursuit of the source of a mysterious black substance that, of course, threatens the future of the world as we know it.

In this scene, Mulder and Scully are driving through the desert, whereupon they come to a dead end in the road. Uncertain of which way to go (left or right), they debate their options before Mulder chooses a third, unexpected option: to go straight and blaze a new trail.

Use this scene to illustrate that in the postmodern experience, there may be previously unforeseen options on our journey of Christian discipleship that take us off the map and lead us to the Truth that longs to be discovered. *(VHS, 56:45–57:52) Total time: 1:07*

Pop Music

Alanis Morissette, "Ironic"

True to the postmodern spiritual experience of Generation X, Morissette embraces one of its key themes—irony. "Life has a funny way of sneaking up on you/Life has a funny, funny way of helping you out/Helping you out."

Aimee Mann, "Save Me"

A plea for salvation from the ranks of those who fear "they could never love anyone."

U2, "Love Rescue Me"

Having conquered his past, and standing at the entrance of a new world, the narrator, once lost, longs to leave the ruins of his life and walk into the future, redeemed and re-dreamed.

R.E.M., "I've Been High"

A man climbs so high in life only to feel so empty, missing the "big reveal." Diving into a pool, he feels life wash over him. He closes his eyes to see that what he believes now believes in him, and he begins to imagine the life he desires to "live on high."

Literature

Dave Eggers, from *A Heartbreaking Work of Staggering Genius*

I am the perfect amalgam! I was born of both stability and chaos. I have seen nothing and everything. I am twenty-four but feel ten thousand years old. I am emboldened by youth, unfettered and hopeful, though inextricably tied to the past and future by my beautiful brother, who is part of both. Can you not see that we're extraordinary? That we were meant for something else, something more...Can you not see what I represent? I am both (a) martyred moralizer and (b) amoral omnivore born of the suburban vacuum + idleness + Catholicism + alcoholism + violence; I am a freak in secondhand velour, a leper who uses L'Oreal Antisticky Mega Gel. I am rootless, ripped from all foundations, an orphan raising an orphan and wanting to take everything there is and replace it with stuff I've made. I have nothing but friends and what's left of my little family. I need community, I need feedback, I need love, connection, give-and-take—I will bleed if they will love me. Let me try. Let me prove.[3]

Images

Water, ponds, friends, and a man in the Super Bowl crowd wearing a red wig and holding the enduring "John 3:16" sign.

Mission

Use this sermon to launch a new small group in the congregation that focuses on community, prayer, and the ancient traditions and practices of our Christian heritage. Recommended resource: *Companions in Christ*, published by Upper Room Books.

Mile Twenty

Luke 4:14–21

He unrolled the scroll and found the place where it was written: "The Spirit of the Lord is upon me, because he has anointed me to bring good news to the poor. He has sent me to proclaim release to the captives and recovery of sight to the blind, to let the oppressed go free, to proclaim the year of the Lord's favor." And he rolled up the scroll, gave it back to the attendant, and sat down. (Luke 4:17b–20a)

Twenty-six point two miles. In the world of running it's what separates the weekend warriors from the real players. It's called the marathon, and those who have crossed its finish line at least once in their lives will tell you that it is, in a very strange sense, a profoundly spiritual experience. It slowly breaks you down, takes you deep into that unexplored territory of your soul where you are all alone with yourself, where all your weaknesses are exposed to you in glaring fashion, where you discover just how fragile you are from head to toe, heart and soul.

When I ran the L.A. Marathon a couple of years ago, I had no idea that there would be thousands of people lining the streets. It seemed as though they were there just for me—children standing on the corners giving me high fives as I ran by, strangers handing me food and water, people of all sizes and colors and languages cheering me and praising me as if, in that moment, I was walking on the moon or walking on water. It's just what you need when you're out there in no-man's-land, when you're too far to turn around and too stupid to know what you've just gotten yourself into. All that hype and support literally propels you toward the next mile marker.

But it ends all too soon. I expected to ride that wave of emotion right to the finish line; but strangely, the closer I drew to the finish line, the quieter the crowd became. Their spirit changed, their enthusiasm waned; you could almost sense that they were not sure if they should cheer for you or cry for you. I remember turning a corner at around mile twenty and overhearing a woman saying to someone, "Oh, my God! Look at that guy." I suddenly felt like a bad accident in the middle of the highway. As they watched us, they seemed less involved and suddenly more distant and removed; they were not so much supporters as they were casual, curious onlookers, perhaps wondering what it must be like to be *them,* and silently thankful that they're not.

For me it was a poignant parable about life. When you're at mile two in your life, you've got more friends than you could ever need; but when you're at mile twenty in your life, the crowd often thins out. Had Jesus been a marathon runner, he might have told the parable about the runner who hits that wall at mile twenty and discovers that there is no one there to lift him up and carry him across the finish line. *The harvest is plenty, but the workers are few.*

That's why Jesus begins his public ministry the way he does. That's the story we just read from the gospel of Luke. It's his first public appearance, and everyone wants to know who this man is, what he stands for, what he's all about. So there in the synagogue, he rises to his feet and gives his inauguration speech. He unrolls the scroll of the prophet Isaiah and goes right to that passage that for thirty years must have been brewing in the depths of his soul. "The spirit of the Lord is upon me," he reads, "because he has anointed me to bring good news to the poor, to proclaim release to the captives and recovery of sight to the blind, to free those who are oppressed, and to proclaim God's favor to the dispossessed."

That's a theology of *the wall.* That's mile twenty theology. That's why I'm here, he says. Because the world lives at mile twenty. At mile twenty the streets are jammed with people who don't think they can go another step, so I'm here to pick them up and carry them across the finish line. I'm here because the world is full of people who have hit the wall in their lives, and they're wondering why those who profess to know the Lord sit quietly on the curbside watching while those in the street languish and stumble.

He preaches a theology of the twentieth mile. Then he rolls up the scroll, walks out the front doors of the church, and heads for mile twenty. And Luke says that before the day was even over, Jesus turns the city of Capernaum on its head with all the healings he was able to do.

The world is living at mile twenty these days. Jesus knew that. He knew that one way or another, we're all at mile twenty. We're either out there on the road, trying to make it home and hitting the wall, or we're out on the curbside watching. He knew that, either way, we need help out at mile twenty. We either need to grab a hand or offer a hand.

In the hit musical *Rent,* there is a scene in which a group of people are arranged in hospital beds on the stage. They are all out at mile twenty, so to speak, living with AIDS and facing a fragile future. Together they sing about their fears of losing their dignity and dying alone, neglected, unwanted. They ask, "Will I wake tomorrow from this nightmare?"

We live in a culture of casual, curious observation in which the nightmares of others become entertainment for the world. Turn on your TV in the afternoon, and you'll see what I mean. We love to be entertained by the misery of others. From Sally and Montel to Judge Judy and Court TV, we are entertained by sin and brokenness and disputes and violence. At mile twenty, we watch from the curb and wait to see how it's all going to turn out. And even when it hits closer to home with the neighbor down the street or the colleague at the office, we often do the same.

In his book *Taste and See,* Tim Dearborn tells of a woman named Grace in his church. For forty years, Grace had an "awe-inspiring" ministry to street people in Seattle. When asked her secret, she replied, "If you want to have ministry on the streets, then walk slowly and it will happen to you. If you want to avoid it, then walk fast."[1]

It's true in all of life. If we are going to follow Jesus Christ and live as his servants in the world, we need to walk slowly through this life, and the opportunities for mercy and compassion will happen to us. Dearborn writes, "All around us are people whose distress we may not be able to see. Often it's carefully hidden. But when we look at the world the way God sees it, the way Jesus sees it today, we are given the gift of his sight, so that we can stop, climb over the walls that divide us, gently touch others and help them to their feet."[2]

In an old farmhouse in Sonoma County, north of San Francisco, lives a group of Catholic monastics—lay people, not ordained—who operate an unconventional hospice for children with HIV. Members of Starcross Community spend their days training others to care for children with AIDS at home, or helping the children with their homework. When a child is sick, they spend many days in the rocking chair with him or her, and many nights rubbing backs or scratching itchy sores to offer what comfort they can. Some of these children, before coming to the community, have never been touched save for twice-daily diaper changes and bottle feedings. So the prescription offered by Starcross is merely one of the fullness of everyday life—the love of family, the security of home, the joy of childhood. In a society in which only long, eventful lives are revered, says Brother Toby, "We must somehow recognize that there is a beauty even in these short lives."[3]

The neighbor on the corner whose wife has just left him, the single mother next door whose ADHD child has nearly pushed her over the edge, the folks in the wheelchairs at the senior center who are lined up in the hallways like broken-down, abandoned cars—will we meet them at the twentieth mile of their lives? Jesus says we will if we want to be his followers. We will walk slowly and interact with the world at mile twenty. We will get involved the way Jesus gets involved in the world—with a hand, a touch, a word, a kiss.

Hubert H. Humphrey once said, "The true moral test of people is how they treat those in the dawn of life—the children; those who are in the twilight of life—the aged; and those who are in the shadow of life—the sick, the needy, the handicapped." Jesus said it is the true moral test of an inner righteousness and the anointing of the Spirit.

Anne Lamott recorded the painfully honest journal of her son's first year of life and the struggles she endured as a single mother and a recovering alcoholic. She writes about a particular day when she had reached the depths of exhaustion and depression and frustration with her newborn son; she had decided, somewhat facetiously, that it was totally crazy to believe in Christ. Then, she writes, something truly amazing happened.

> A man from church showed up at the front door, smiling and waving at Sam, and I went to let him in. He is a white man named Gordon, fiftyish, married to our associate pastor, and after exchanging pleasantries he said, "Margaret and I wanted to do something for you and the baby. So what I want to ask is, 'What if a fairy appeared on your doorstep and said that she would do any favor for you at all, anything you wanted around the house that you felt too exhausted to do by yourself and too ashamed to ask someone else to help you with?'"

> "I can't even say," I said. "It's too horrible."
>
> But he finally convinced me to tell him, and I said it would be to clean the bathroom, and he ended up spending an hour scrubbing the bathtub and toilet and sink with Ajax and hot water. I sat on the couch while he worked, watching TV, nursing Sam to sleep, and feeling very guilty. But it made me feel sure of Christ again, of that kind of love. This, a man scrubbing a new mother's bathtub, is what Jesus means to me.[4]

It's what Jesus intended to do. And he told us that if we intend to follow him, so will we. We'll meet him out at mile twenty, where he'll hand us the tools of the trade—eyes to see, hands to heal, words to speak, life to give.

ART GALLERY

Major Motion Picture Clips

The Apostle (1997). After being squeezed out of his church by his ex-wife, a Texas fundamentalist preacher's alcohol-fueled rage sends him off the deep end. After beating her new beau into a coma, he flees to Louisiana and seizes the chance to reinvent himself as a devout "apostle," founding a new church and captivating the citizenry while keeping his sins buried.

In this clip, when a man arrives at his church to bulldoze it, the apostle E. F. (Robert Duvall) reaches out to him and leads him to a dramatic conversion. This entire scene may be too lengthy to use within a sermon; choose an appropriate time to cut it. *(VHS, 1:39:02–1:47:05) Total time: 8:03.*

Pop Music

Phil Collins, "Another Day in Paradise"

A woman in need calls out to a man on the street for help, but he walks on, pretending not to hear. "Oh lord, is there nothing more anybody can do/Oh lord, there must be something you can say..."

R.E.M., "Everybody Hurts"

A plea to hold on in the longest, loneliest night, and "take comfort in your friends."

Literature

William Styron, ***Darkness Visible: A Memoir of Madness***

> It is of great importance that those who are suffering a siege [of depression], perhaps for the first time, be told—be convinced, rather—that the illness will run its course and that they will pull through. A tough job, this; calling "Chin up!" from the safety of the shore to a drowning person is tantamount to insult, but it has been shown over and over again that if the encouragement is dogged enough—and the support equally committed and passionate—the endangered one can nearly always be saved. Most people in the grip of depression at its ghastliest are, for whatever reason, in a state of unrealistic hopelessness, torn by exaggerated ills and fatal threats that bear no resemblance to actuality. It may require on the part of friends, lovers, family, admirers, an almost religious devotion to persuade the sufferers of life's worth, which is so often in conflict with a sense of their own worthlessness, but such devotion has prevented countless suicides.[5]

Images

Marathon runners, street intersections, open roads, inner-city streetscapes.

Mission

I used this sermon to launch a new ministry in the congregation called "Mile Twenty," a care team of laypersons who committed themselves to eight months of intensive training in the areas of prayer, skilled helping, hospital visitation, crisis intervention, and listening. Eighteen laypersons responded to the call to serve in this vital ministry and were commissioned for ministry later that year.

Consider developing a program that is indigenous to your congregation's needs and skill sets, or explore the possibility of the highly successful Stephen Ministry program.

Our Father...

Matthew 6:7–13

"Pray then in this way: Our Father in heaven..." (Matthew 6:9)

A mother was teaching her six-year-old daughter how to pray the Lord's Prayer. Every night before bedtime, she'd sit down with her and go over the words, and every night the little girl would memorize a little more of the prayer. Then it happened one night that she said, "Mom, I think I can do this on my own." And she recited the prayer, beautifully, without skipping a beat, until she came near the end of the prayer, where she said, "And lead us not into temptation, but deliver us from e-mail."

We all need a little help with this prayer, don't we? Here's a prayer that we pray every Sunday in church. It's a prayer that many Christians pray every day. We know it like the back of our hand; it's about as routine as the Pledge of Allegiance; it has become a part of the fabric of our spiritual lives.

But do we know what we're praying? Do we really know what we are doing when we toss these words around? When we pray these words, it's like we're playing with a load of TNT. Uttering this prayer is one of the most radical, revolutionary acts a Christian can do in this world. As Frederick Buechner says, to pray this prayer is to "unleash a power that makes atomic power look like a warm breeze."[1]

The Lord's Prayer is a big, hairy, audacious prayer. But it begins with the two simple words that make it bearable—*Our Father*. With those very words we are reminded that we stand in the presence of the One who hears us, knows us as his own, and longs to be in relationship with us in ways that transcend even our purest relationships with others here on this earth.

Our Father. There's so much power in those words, but there's a lot of confusion, too, especially with that second word—*Father*. Many of us struggle with that word because, for some reason or other, we struggled with our earthly fathers. Take my generation, for instance—Generation X. It's believed that 30 percent of my generation grew up without a father in their lives; 50 percent grew up in broken families in which their fathers played a less active role in their lives. So there's a lot of pain there when we say the word *Father.*

The rock band Everclear speaks of that pain in one of their hit songs, "Father of Mine," in which the narrator asks his biological father where he's been and how it is possible for a father to simply disappear from a child's life. Not knowing where his father has gone, and pronouncing judgment on his father's wasted life, he confesses, "My dad, he gave me a name, and then he walked away."

We have to be honest about that kind of pain if we're going to pray to the God we call Father. We also have to somehow get past it, because God is not that kind of father, nor is he very much like even the best father we can ever have or imagine.

We encounter a new image of the Father when we read the Bible, one that goes beyond our experience of our earthly fathers. It comes from the book of Exodus, the fourth chapter. You'll find there the story of Moses, who is called by God to go before Pharaoh. Now you'll recall that Pharaoh is the king of Egypt. He holds all of God's people in slavery, right? And God is not going to allow that. God has a plan for his people, and slavery is not part of it. So he calls Moses and says to him, "I want you to go before Pharaoh, and I want you to deliver a message to him. 'Thus says the Lord: Israel is my firstborn son. Let my son go so that he may worship me'" (Ex. 4:22–23, paraphrased)

Now what makes this passage so significant to what we're talking about today is that it represents the very first time in all of scripture that God identifies himself as a Father or parent of a child.[2] Up to this point in the biblical story we know God in scripture as Creator—the one who made all things in heaven and earth. Some people stick with that metaphor and never get beyond it. I hear it far too often: Why go to church when I can go out on the hilltop or down to the beach and watch the sunset and meet God there? And it's true—you can know something about who the artist is by admiring his art. But the metaphor only goes so far. I happen to admire the work of the great Russian artist Marc Chagall, but I never knew Marc Chagall. If I could collect every piece of Chagall's artwork and fill the walls of my house and admire his work daily, I would still not know him. And the truth is that I'd rather have Mark Chagall in my house than have one of his paintings on my wall.

God understood this. He wanted his people to know him, not just know about him. He wanted his people to speak *to* him rather than simply to speak *about* him. So God gets involved in a deeper way. For the first time in Scripture he calls us his children, calls himself our Father. And he describes the nature of his role as the father of Israel. Here in Exodus, he says his role, his personal mission, is to free his children. And so from here on out, whenever Israel calls God "Father," it is calling out to the God whose most treasured dream for his children is that they are free—free from slavery, free from the ball and chain, free from the claims that the world puts on them, free from the Pharaohs of this world. When we pray to God the Father, we are praying to the One who has the power to set us free. That's the job of the Father; that's what he does—he works for our freedom.

That's why, when Jesus sits alone in the Garden of Gethsemane, he prays these powerful words: "Father, if you are willing, remove this cup from me; yet, not my will but yours be done" (Lk. 22:42). Jesus is praying to the One who promises to save him from the powers of this world, and he knows that even if this burden does not pass from him, the burden will not own him.

So we pray these words, "Our Father." And when we do, we are talking to the One who calls us his children, the One who promises us that when we call him Father, and live as his children, he will work to free us from whatever it is that keeps us from him.

What is that in your life? What is it that the Father wants to free you from? What Pharaoh is rattling your chains? The Father wants you free from it. That's his mission—to get you back. And Christians hold to the core confession that in Jesus Christ, he's already put up the ransom.

We call it *sin,* this Pharaoh, and that is a tough word for our generation. It's a loaded word, with a diversity of meanings for different people in different circumstance; but I want us to be honest about it, because I want you to be able to talk to God, and God wants you to be honest with him when you talk with him.

What is sin? Paul Tillich suggests that sin, at its most fundamental level, is experienced as estrangement, or separation. As we read the biblical narrative, we encounter at least two expressions of separation: separation from God and separation from one another. Consider the Ten Commandments, which talk about the sins we commonly understand as transgressions in our relationship with God: putting other gods before YHWH, using God's name in vain for our own purposes, forgetting to honor God on the Sabbath by resting one day out of the week. What are these about? They're about separation from God. And the other commandments—murder, adultery, stealing, bearing false witness against another person, and coveting your neighbor's powerboat—what are these about? While they reflect a degree of separation between humanity and God, they are principally concerned with the separation we experience in our relationships with others.

God the Father wants us back; he longs to bring home those who are separated from him and from one another. When the man comes to Jesus and asks him, "What is the greatest commandment?" Jesus says, "'You shall love the Lord your God with all your heart, and with all your soul, and with all your mind.' This is the greatest and first commandment. And a second is like it: 'You shall love your neighbor as yourself'" (Mt. 22:37–39). Do you see this? It's about living in a right and just relationship with God and neighbor. This is the biblical theology of sin and redemption. Sin as separation, and the reconciliation of God through Jesus Christ as the redemptive glue that holds us together.

This is why, when we pray, we pray these words: "Our Father." Not "My Father," but "*Our* Father." We are not alone in praying; if we are alone, then we are not free, and our prayer is dishonest. When we pray, if we are honest in that act of prayer, we are not separated from God or from our neighbors.

Having been raised Catholic, my family had a ritual every Sunday in church. When it came time to pray the Lord's Prayer, we would hold hands, all four of us. At the time I never understood why we did this, other than that it woke me up or kept me from scratching the enamel off the pew. We'd pray, "Our Father..." and there we were, holding hands. Only now do I understand why. My parents seemed to understand that when we pray as Christians, there is no separation between us. God's children look like a family, act like a family, pray like a family. We did this for years. Even when I was sixteen and I had a reputation to worry about. Even when I was seventeen and would bring my girlfriend, who would later become my wife, to church, my father would reach over and grab her hand, and I would blush. It became part of our heritage as a family. Years later, on my father's last day of life, we gathered in a hospital room, held hands, and prayed, "Our Father..."

There is no separation when we pray that prayer in honesty. God wants to deliver us all, together. And the truth about that prayer is that none of us can be entirely free unless all of us are free.

The memoir by J. D. Dolan entitled *Phoenix* is about the pain and struggle that families go through: the separation, the sin, and how these things get passed down from father to son, from generation to generation. The story is about J. D.'s older brother, John, who was burned over 90 percent of his body in a deadly explosion at a Southern California Edison power plant in the Mojave Desert in 1985. Several men died in the explosion, and John was clinging to life in a burn unit in Phoenix, Arizona. J. D. hadn't spoken to his dying brother in more than five years, which was how the Dolan family dealt with disagreements over the years. His father hadn't spoken to his daughter in more than ten years, and now J. D.'s brother was dealing out the same punishment with him. Only now John lay unconscious, dying, and J. D. holds vigil for weeks over his brother's bedside, searching for words. He wants to tell his brother that it is OK to die, but he's not even sure if his brother can hear him; or if he can hear him, will he want his brother to break the silence after so many years?

It is an agonizing witness to the power of Pharaoh in one family's life. J. D. twists and turns in the wind for days, until finally resolving to speak the words of forgiveness and grace that must be spoken before his brother dies.

> It occurred to me that I wasn't mad at my brother anymore, and I knew that in the end, when it mattered, he wasn't mad at me. And I knew that I loved him very much, and that he loved me. And in this there was considerable grace.
>
> On the longest day of the year, I told my brother that he was going to die. I don't imagine he heard me and I don't even remember what I said—but I do remember a kind of clearing. I stopped crying and leaned close to him, and I said, softly, clearly, "Hey, buddy."[3]

That's what it takes to pray "Our Father." The courage to be free—freed by God the Father who demands that Pharaoh let his children go so that we might be free to love the Father with all our heart and soul and mind, and to love one another the way we love ourselves.

"For you did not receive a spirit of slavery to fall back into fear, but you have received a spirit of adoption [whereby] we cry, 'Abba! Father!'" (Rom. 8:15).

ART GALLERY

Major Motion Picture Clips

Clip 1: Prayer is one of the most radical deeds of the Christian life. For many, it's also one of the most terrifying. The preacher would do well to speak to this fear and invite the hearers to laugh at their own awkward experiences of finding the right words at the right moment. I suggest using a video clip from the movie *Meet the Parents* (2000) to introduce the sermon theme. This could be used at the start of worship or just prior to the sermon.

In this clip, Greg Focker (Ben Stiller) has just met his future in-laws. After a disastrous introduction, he sits down at the dinner table, whereupon his future father-in-law, Jack (Robert De Niro), invites him to pray before the meal. The hilarious, rambling petition that follows is both brilliantly entertaining and painfully true.

Begin the clip with Jack's request, "Greg, would you like to say grace?" and end with Jack's curious response, "Thank you, Greg, that was interesting too." *(VHS, 0:24:28–0:26:15) Total time: 1:47.*

Clip 2: In this sermon I have been intentional about leading the hearers to a moment of grace and a subtle, yet unmistakable, call to reconciliation with those from whom they are estranged. In lieu of the selection from Dolan's *Phoenix,* the preacher may choose to use a very powerful, emotionally charged clip from the movie *Being Human* (1994), starring Robin Williams. The entire film consists of five parables, set in five different eras of human history, each of which tell the story of a man, Hector, who has, either by his own personal choices or by circumstances beyond his control, become estranged from those he loves.

In this clip, Williams plays the role of a present-day deadbeat father who, after a painful divorce, has left his children entirely to the care of their mother. After an unexplained absence of several years, he returns home and convinces his children to spend the weekend with him at a beach house retreat. Over dinner he describes to them the painful journey that took him away and his genuine, humble desire to be reunited with them.

Begin the clip with the opening scene at the restaurant: "Lots of people get divorced..." End with Hector and the daughter walking out together: "It's all right. It doesn't matter. It's past. I'm a lifesaver now." *(VHS, 1:45:00–1:49:00) Total time: 5:00.*

"Man on the Street"

With a video camera and a microphone, interview people on the street or in the local mall, or people in your church, seeking responses to the following questions:

> If you could say "I love you" to one person in your life, who would it be, and why?
>
> If you could say "I'm sorry" to one person in your life, who would it be, and why?

Edit the selections, with careful attention to diversity, humor, and honesty, and present a short clip (two minutes) at the end of the sermon, or as a call to worship, or both.

Pop Music

For a powerful conclusion to the sermon, invite the worship music team to perform "Living Years," written and performed by Mike and the Mechanics (Atlantic Recording Corp., 1988). Secure permission to publicly project the lyrics on screen, and display the lyrics, line by line, as they are sung.

The narrator reaches a moment of clarity in his life about the unresolved brokenness in his relationship with his dead father, realizing that blame is passed from generation to generation, holding us hostage to the past and precluding us from moving forward with our lives despite our disagreements. He reflects on all that could have been said, all that could have been done, to overcome the bitterness and heal the wounds and gain a new perspective. It's not until he looks into the face of his newborn baby that he realizes what he wanted to say to his father before his death, confessing—*"I just wish I could have told him in the living years."*

Images

To enhance the worship experience and strengthen the theme of reconciliation and freedom from broken relationships, consider using supporting images on the screen throughout the entire service, especially during the suggested musical performance of "Living Years."

Suggested images: parents with children, single parents, grandparents holding babies, family reunions, couples holding hands. Try to avoid the Norman Rockwell–like portrayal of families; these images should be honest about human relationships in all of their complex, intimate expressions.

Mission

This sermon may provide an opportunity to establish a small group study or congregational workshop on the Christian practice of prayer. Consider many possible resources, such as Martha Rowlett's *Responding to God: A Guide to Daily Prayer* (Nashville: Upper Room Books, 1999), which includes guides for both leaders and participants.

Partly Cloudy, Chance of Rain

2 Samuel 11:1—12:7

In the spring of the year, the time when kings go out to battle, David sent Joab with his officers and all Israel with him; they ravaged the Ammonites, and besieged Rabbah. But David remained at Jerusalem. (2 Samuel 11:1)

From the Associated Press comes the story of a recent major archaeological discovery in China. Chinese researchers have discovered, much to their surprise, a two-thousand-year-old toilet, complete with running water, a stone seat, and a comfortable armrest. Archaeologists found the antique facility in, among all places, the tomb of a certain king of the Western Han Dynasty, dated some time between 206 B.C. and A.D. 24. The king apparently believed his soul would need to make a pit stop even after bodily death, so he went to the grave prepared. The archaeologists were amazed not only by the sophistication of this facility but also by its remarkable resemblance to the modern-day facilities that all of us enjoy in our homes today, evidenced in particular by the upward position in which the king left the seat and the small stack of *Reader's Digest* magazines they discovered near the unit. The only remaining question, the only unsolved mystery these archaeologists could not resolve, pertained, of course, to the age-old dilemma: Does the roll pull from the bottom or from over the top? The old king, in his haste, forgot to reload.

Imagine spending all that time and effort digging through ancient Chinese ruins, watching your colleagues as they uncover precious jewels, ancient pottery, weathered scrolls, and highly coveted religious relics; and you're the lucky one who unearths, of all things, a primitive toilet that belonged to an old, cranky king. What are the chances of that? Imagine all the dinner parties where curious friends are asking you what you discovered over in China; imagine trying to keep a straight face while you try, unconvincingly, to explain the glory of your job.

Life has a funny way of doing that to us. You don't always find what you're looking for. There are some things you'd rather not find. There are times when you go looking for jewels in life and you get the old king's toilet instead. You say to yourself, "You know, I could have gone all day without having discovered that."

The Bible is a lot like that. We go looking through the Bible for jewels, little pearls of wisdom and hope and traditional family values, stories that are all cleaned up with no sticky mess, no dirt. But every once in a while we come across a story in the Bible that is so full of scandal and sin and deceit and despair that we can't help but blush and wish it would go away.

The story of David and Bathsheba makes the afternoon soaps look like *Sesame Street.* We call it the story of David and Bathsheba, but it's really a story about David, the king, the hero of all of Israel, the giant-killer, the musician, the songwriter, God's anointed one. It's a story about the greatest hero in Israel's history who goes to great lengths to get what isn't his, and who goes to even greater lengths to undo what cannot be undone. And because it's a story about the real world and real people, it's a story about you and me and all of us here. It becomes a window through which we see the world in all of its brokenness. And if we dare to look through that window long and hard enough, we will see not only the outside world but also, when the sunlight hits the window at just the right angle, a reflection of ourselves, in all of our brokenness and failings. And when that happens, the story not only is more than we want to know about David but also becomes more than we can bear to comprehend about ourselves.

While Israel's army is off conquering and plundering and pillaging the Ammonites in the name of God, David is quietly walking the roof of his palace, talking to his general, Joab, on his cell phone, taking notes on his new Palm Pilot, planning the army's next move via weather reports on the World Wide Web, when all at once he glances down and sees a beautiful woman bathing. He takes one look at her and he knows he cannot live without her. And he knows that he *can* have her because he is a powerful man. So he sends for her.

The scripture says simply, "He sent for her, she came to him, and he lay with her. Then she went home." That's it. No red merlot, no dancing, no romancing. It was over before it ever really started. David got what he wanted, got what he couldn't live without, and was done with her. But she wasn't done with him, because it isn't long after that fateful encounter that she sends him an e-mail. "I'm pregnant," reads the subject line.

David does not panic. He's fought bigger giants than this before. He can handle this. He goes immediately to Plan A, which is to make the problem quietly go away. His solution is one of minimal cost: Arrange for Uriah to get together with Bathsheba, and no one will ever question the issue of paternity. But Uriah, unlike David, was off at war. David calls Joab and orders him to send Uriah home. And when Uriah arrives, David calls him in and orders him to go home and get reacquainted with his wife, but Uriah is a man of principle who takes his oath of wartime celibacy seriously. Uriah will not do the deed. The following day, David throws a party, sees to it that Uriah gets drunk, and sends him home. But Uriah, even in his altered state, is a man of integrity; he refuses to go home.

You can already see the incredible contrast of moral character between David, the anointed one of God, and Uriah, who isn't even an Israelite, but a mere Hittite. So far David has broken three commandments: He has *coveted* his neighbor's wife; he has *stolen* what belongs to Uriah; and he has committed *adultery*. But there is more.

Plan B. David speed-dials Joab, tells Joab that Uriah is on his way back to war, and when he arrives in camp, Uriah is to go straight to the forefront of the battle, where the fighting is most fierce; then Joab is to draw back, leaving Uriah out in no-man's-land, and see to it that he is killed. Joab is a man of swift expediency; he doesn't ask questions; he simply follows orders. What David orders is exactly what Joab does. Uriah is struck down and killed. The final deed is done, and another commandment is broken. David is now a thief, an adulterer, and a *murderer,* but David has saved his own hide. And when the threatening storm clouds seemingly blow through for David, he takes Bathsheba as his wife, and she bears him a son.

In the movie *Magnolia,* various weather reports flash on the screen throughout the three-hour film. The first weather report, at the beginning of the film, reads, "Partly cloudy, 82% chance of rain." With that report, you know that a certain storm is on the way in this movie, and that nine of the main characters in the movie, each of whom are desperately broken and lost, are all heading toward a sudden and devastating downpour in their lives.

It's about to pour down hard on David at this point in the story. It appears that he's dodged the bullet and averted a personal scandal with devastating consequences for himself and for Israel. Once again the king has killed a giant problem. But an unavoidable storm is brewing for David, and it will rain down hard on his life. He is through with his past, but his past is not through with him.

David's story reveals at least three unmistakable truths about human behavior in the face of sin, three ominous clouds that invariably lead to crushing downpours and devastating floods in our lives.

Hovering over David's life from the very outset of the story is the looming *cloud of aloneness*. The whole drama of the story begins with David alone on his rooftop when his role as the leader of Israel requires him to be out with his soldiers at war. "David remained at Jerusalem," (2 Sam. 11:1). As Walter Brueggemann suggests, "David was not in the action but stays behind to initiate other action."[1] He is all alone, and it's in his aloneness that the silent desires of his heart are let out of the cage in the absence of anyone who could hold him accountable for his actions.

The old proverb is true: "One is the loneliest number that you'll ever know." When we live independent and autonomous lives without anyone else to challenge and question our intentions and our actions, we are so vulnerable to sin. The story of Jesus in the wilderness, the showdown in the desert, shows us the truth of that. It's not until Jesus is all alone that the evil one pays him a visit and tempts him with all the power and control and fame one could ever want or need. Jesus battles the evil one alone, and he conquers that temptation, but even then, God sends angels to minister to him in that hour.

But there are others in scripture who are not so fortunate. I think of Judas, all alone in his scheming, all alone in his silent act of betrayal; had he shared the secret desires of his heart with Peter, with James or John, with Jesus, perhaps he would have come to his senses.

I think of Peter too. After Judas has done his irrevocable deed and Jesus is led away from Gethsemane, Peter is alone downtown, warming his hands over the fire, and the stranger says, "Aren't you one of them?" Wandering outside of his community of accountability and support, Peter knows a depth of personal weakness he never before thought possible.

I think of the rich young ruler, as he is called in the gospels, who seemingly has everything there is to get in this world, yet is so spiritually bankrupt he cannot for the life of him give it all up to gain the very thing he cannot live without. Jesus offers him the kingdom if only he will sell all he has to give to the needs of the poor. For two thousand years, he's been stuck in the eye of the needle, alone.

There's a reason why on the TV show *Who Wants to Be a Millionaire?* Regis gave the options to poll the audience or phone a friend. Friends can save us. Friends can show us things we wouldn't or couldn't see on our own. Friends can hold us accountable when the dark desires of our heart become more than we can bear alone.

That's why Jesus sent his disciples out two by two. Jesus had firsthand knowledge of what life alone in the wilderness was like, so he set up a way to be in ministry so that we wouldn't be defenseless in the face of temptation.

The truth of our life in Christ is that we all need human lifelines. We all need someone to whom we can turn in those hard moments when the evil one comes knocking on our door, when temptation shows its teeth. "In...the time when kings go out to battle...David remained at Jerusalem" (v. 1). Everyone who was someone was out of town. David was alone.

In David's story the cloud of aloneness gives rise to the *cloud of shameless desperation.* As the story unravels and David loses control, he goes to any length to cover his sin, even to the point of murder. The more he loses control of his situation, the further he wanders from the presence of God. Cut adrift from the anchor of God's purpose for his life, he's pulled deeper and deeper into dangerous waters. As the shoreline slowly fades from sight, there is nothing he won't do to undo what's been done.

"It is an old ironic habit of humans to run faster when we are lost," said Rollo May. When things slip through our hands, we're prone to grasp even more tightly. In David's case, his act of shameless desperation is to get Joab involved, to drag him into the mud of his own sin. David turns to Joab, his hatchet man, the one whose job it is to do what the king says without second-guessing, without reservation.

It's been said that a drowning man is difficult to rescue without the rescuer being pulled under with him. He loses all awareness of his situation, is concerned solely with his own survival; he'll do anything to make it out in one piece. The deeper into sin we spin, the more devastating the consequences of our sin become, not only for us, but for those around us. Jesus reminds us that when we cause others to stumble, our sin grows exponentially. What we do to ourselves we do to the entire web of life.

David can't stop. In the sticky web of his own sin, Joab and all of Israel is unwittingly caught with him. And the storm builds as the *cloud of denial* hovers above. Now that Joab is brought into the fray with the death of Uriah, David says to him, "Do not let this matter trouble you" (v. 25). It's nothing, he says. These kinds of things happen in war. That's just life.

We do that, don't we? We can rationalize just about anything in order to put it behind us and move on. In the face of our sinfulness, we see only what we want to see.

I read recently that employees at Microsoft are prohibited from using the word *bug* when referring to software failures. At Microsoft, they don't have bugs; they have what they call *issues.* That sounds a whole lot better, cleaner, doesn't it? I'm not dealing with failure, we say; it's not sin I'm struggling with. I'm just working through some *issues* in my life, we say.

But "if we say that we have no sin, we deceive ourselves, and the truth is not in us" (1 Jn. 1:8). It's another way of saying, "Deal with it." Not "get over it," not "get by with it," not "get past it," but "deal with it, face it," because while we may be done with our past, our past isn't done with us.

The only way to stop chasing our own shadow is to turn and face the sun in all of its terrifying, fiery light. To name the darkness that holds us, to expose the devastation we've worked so hard to conceal, to face our culpability and our utter inability to free ourselves from it on our own. It takes perhaps more courage to do that than any of us would dare believe possible, but Nathan is on his way to help us face the truth and come to the light. He cannot save us from the inevitable downpour, but he also will not allow us to be swept away only to drown. He comes not to sink us, but to save us; not to condemn us, but to transform us. "You are the man," he declares.

It is the clashing of thunder and cracking of light, that word of God. And with the thunder and lightning comes the awful rain, and with the rain comes the painful revelation, the terrifying truth that leads to the way out, the way up, the way home.

We may be done with our past, but our past is not done with us. That sounds a lot like judgment to those on the run; but for those who can no longer keep up the frantic pace, it is the dawning of grace and the beginning of a brand new day.

ART GALLERY

Major Motion Picture Clips

Clip 1: After setting up the spiritual imagery of the inevitable downpour, cut to a video clip from the movie *Magnolia* (1999).

In this clip, as the spiritually broken characters of the film each come to an awareness of the devastating consequences of their choices, the ominous storm finally unleashes its fury, not with a downpour of water, but of frogs (a dramatic re-creation of the story of the plague of frogs, as described in Exodus). Begin the clip with Jimmy Gator in the kitchen, preparing to take his life, before a falling frog breaks through the glass window and knocks the gun from his hands. End when the storm finally breaks, or when appropriate *(VHS, 02:30:00–02:34:00) Total time: 4:00.*

Clip 2: Begin the worship experience by playing a clip from U2's *Rattle and Hum* (1988), in which the band performs the song "I Still Haven't Found What I'm Looking For." Filmed live in an African American church in Harlem and supported musically by a black gospel choir, this song addresses the spiritual angst of our generation and the daily struggle of living between grace and sin. *(VHS, 0:15:49–0:19:46) Total time: 3:57.*

"Man on the Street"

Send a video team into the local community to interview people on the street, seeking responses to the following questions:

Who is your best friend, and why?

Describe your spiritual weather forecast (i.e., sunny and warm, partly cloudy, chance of clearing, 100 percent chance of rain, etc.).

Edit the selections, with careful attention to diversity, humor, and honesty, and present a short clip (two minutes) before the sermon, or at another appropriate time during the worship service.

Pop Music

For a dramatic, reflective conclusion to the sermon, invite a soloist to sing Aimee Mann's haunting, graceful song, "Wise Up" (Reprise Records, 1999). With permission, prepare the lyrics for screen projection and present the lyrics on the screen, line by line, as they are sung. For a multisensory experience, layer the lyrics over video footage of storms, lightning, or dark clouds.

It's not what you thought,
When you first began it
You got what you want
You can hardly stand it, though
By now you know it's not going to stop
It's not going to stop
It's not going to stop
'Til you wise up

You're sure there's a cure
And you have finally found it
You think one drink
Will shrink you 'til you're underground
And living down
But it's not going to stop
It's not going to stop
It's not going to stop
'Til you wise up

Prepare a list for what you need
Before you sign away the deed
'Cause it's not going to stop
It's not going to stop
No, it's not going to stop
'til you wise up
No, it's not going to stop
'til you wise up
No, it's not going to stop
So just give up

Another possibility is U2's "Desire."

Images

Clouds, rain, extreme weather, men and women standing in a downpour.

Mission

This sermon may provide an opportunity for hearers to join a small group, a covenant/accountability group, or support group/twelve-step group within the local church. Due to the sermon's strong emphasis on relationships and personal accountability, hearers may feel the call of God to move into a small, intimate, caring community where the work of personal healing, accountability, and restoration can begin.

The church may also choose to arrange for a service of healing and repentance at an alternate time for those in the congregation who feel called by God to move toward forgiveness and reconciliation with God.

Ready for Prime Time

Luke 9:57–62

As they were going along the road, someone said to him, "I will follow you wherever you go." And Jesus said to him, "Foxes have holes, and birds of the air have nests; but the Son of Man has nowhere to lay his head." To another he said, "Follow me." But he said, "Lord, first let me go and bury my father." But Jesus said to him, "Let the dead bury their own dead; but as for you, go and proclaim the kingdom of God." Another said, "I will follow you, Lord; but let me first say farewell to those at my home." Jesus said to him, "No one who puts a hand to the plow and looks back is fit for the kingdom of God." (Luke 9:57–62)

George Saunders, in his *Pastoralia,* writes a brilliant short story about a man named Morse who wishes above all else that he could be someone else—to just be *somebody, anybody,* somebody *other* than himself, whom he considers a *nobody.*

> Morse was tall and thin and as gray and sepulchral as a church about to be condemned. His pants were too short, and his face periodically broke into a tense, involuntary grin that quickly receded, as if he had just suffered a sharp pain. At work he was known to punctuate his conversations with brief wild laughs and gusts of inchoate enthusiasm and subsequent embarrassment...
>
> When he got home, he would sit on the steps and enjoy a few minutes of centered breathing while reciting his mantra, which was Calm Down Calm Down, before the kids came running out and grabbed his legs and sometimes even bit him quite hard in their excitement and Ruth came out to remind him in an angry tone that he wasn't the only one who'd worked all day...
>
> Boy oh boy, could life be a torture. Could life even force a fellow into a strange, dark place from which he found

> himself doing graceless, unforgivable things...If only he could escape BlasCorp and do something significant, such as discover a critical vaccine. But it was too late, and he had never been good at biology and in fact had flunked it twice. But some kind of moment in the sun would certainly not be unwelcome. If only he could be a tortured prisoner of war who not only refused to talk but led the other prisoners in rousing hymns at great personal risk. If only he could witness an actual miracle or save the president from an assassin or win the Lotto and give it all to charity…His childhood dreams had been so bright, he had hoped for so much, it couldn't be true he was a nobody, although, on the other hand, what kind of somebody spends the best years of his life swearing at a photocopier?
>
> [Walking home from work along the river bank, thinking about these things] Morse stopped in his tracks, wondering what in the world two little girls were doing alone in a canoe speeding toward the Falls, apparently oarless...
>
> There was no time...He had just decided that...And swimming was out of the question. Therefore the girls would die. They were basically dead. Although that couldn't be. That was too sad...What to do? He fiercely wished himself elsewhere. The girls saw him now and with their hands appeared to be trying to explain that they would be dead soon...Was he their father? Did they think he was Christ? They were dead, as dead as the ancient dead, and he was needed at home, it was a no-brainer, no one could possibly blame him for this one, and making a low sound of despair in his throat he kicked off his loafers and threw his long ugly body out across the water.[1]

"We could be heroes, just for one day," according to the Wallflowers. Ordinary people doing extraordinary things. "Nobodies" becoming "somebodies." And not just for one day, but for a lifetime.

We could, you know? We could be heroes. Jesus can take an ordinary *Morse* from the riverbank and make him as extraordinary as *William Wallace* in the highlands. It *is* possible. It is *very* possible. But I will tell you something—something you may not want to hear. It *is* possible, but it is *very* unlikely.

We *could* be heroes. But *will* we?

They all came that day. Heard that Jesus was coming through town on tour. So they lined up along the sidewalks waiting for their one shot at glory, their lucky break, their one chance at going prime time with the star of the show. They cleaned themselves up. Brought along their resumes. Wore their Sunday best, just in case He picked them out of the crowd and made them into "somebodies."

Turns out that it was sort of like hoping to win the Lotto despite not having bought a ticket. Oh, don't get me wrong, Jesus *called* their number—"You," he said, "and you over there in the green jacket, and yes, you, with the purple hair, follow me." He called their number. That wasn't the problem. Jesus did his part. The problem was that the people whom he called weren't as ready as they thought they were.

They scheduled the interview. They showed up. They were in the right place at the right time. But they didn't get the job.

They could be heroes, for a lifetime. But they weren't, not even for a day.

They had some pretty good excuses. Jesus says, "Follow me," and the man says, "Okay, sounds good, but let me check my Palm Pilot first, just to make sure it fits into my schedule." Jesus says, "Follow me," and she says, "Hmmm, I think I can fit you in between the tennis game and bunco." Jesus says, "Follow me," and the kid says, "Wait a minute, okay, I'm burning CDs and hanging in a chat room with a girl in Frisco"; the man says, "Can we do it at 3:30, after my golf game"; the woman says, "Okay, right after the swap meet, I'll see what I can do."

They could have been heroes. Jesus is heading for Jerusalem, after all. He is going to die in Jerusalem. He knows that. So he's looking for someone to take with him, someone to join the inner circle, someone to whom he can give the keys to his office after he checks out. They could have been heroes. But they weren't ready for prime time. They could have been followers. But they chose instead to be mere admirers.

I wonder when the heroic moment will come in my life when I will serve something other than myself. My five-year-old son asks me to play catch in the front yard. I say, "Just a minute, buddy." I'll get to that some day. Once I accomplish the heroic things in life, I say, I'm going to see what I can do about that someday.

A homeless man comes into the office looking for some food. I give him some grocery certificates and a bus pass. After he leaves, I head out for *lunch*. Working on my tuna sandwich, alone, I wonder when God will ever give me something heroic to do.

We *could* be heroes. But Jesus knows. He knows.

To be a hero, you have to serve. That's the whole point of this passage from Luke. You have to serve something, someone, other than yourself. And Jesus knows that's tough for us. I think it's even tougher for us today. I've been seeing this license plate frame on cars for years now. I won't mention the church that produces these things. But I'll tell you what it says. I saw one on the back of a brand new Beamer the other day. It said, "You matter to God." Now, I don't dispute that claim. It's gospel theology, to be sure. I just don't think it's the whole gospel. It's part of the gospel. But the rest of the gospel, the offensive, scandalous part, reminds me that it's not all about me. Disciples, says Jesus, need to get over themselves, to turn our attention away from self and its individual, self-absorbed needs, and look toward God and the world he desires to redeem. Anne Lamott puts it another way. She says, "To be engrossed by something outside ourselves is a powerful antidote for the rational mind, the mind that so frequently has its head up its own ass—seeing things in such a narrow and darkly narcissistic way that it presents a colorectal theology, offering hope to no one."[2]

God's universe doesn't revolve around me, as much as I like to think it does. I want to produce my own church license plate frames. They are going to read, "God matters." It's all about God. *God matters*. Christians don't serve themselves. They serve God. That's what makes them heroic. Christians don't give much thought to whether they matter. Jesus didn't. Jesus says, "I've come not to be served but to serve." Jesus says, "The first must be last." Jesus says, "The least among you are the greatest." He says, "If any man would come after me, let him deny himself and take up his cross and follow." That's a far cry from, "You matter to God." Jesus seems to be saying, "God matters. Let's just start with that."

Remember that catchy "Footprints" poem? It's been around the block a few times now. The man dreams about walking along the beach, and for the longest time he sees two sets of footprints, right? God is apparently walking with him. Then at a time when things are going wrong he sees only one set of footprints, so he pulls God aside, right? "Where are you?" he asks God. "Where have you been? I've been all alone out here." And God says, "Hey, zip it. Those are my footprints. I was carrying you."

There's a GenX version of that poem:

One night I had a wondrous dream,
One set of footprints there was seen,
The footprints of my precious Lord,
But mine were not along the shore.

But then some strange prints appeared,
And I asked the Lord, "What have we here?"
Those prints are large and round and neat,
"But Lord, they are too big for feet."

"My child," He said in somber tones,
"For miles I carried you along.
I challenged you to walk in faith,
But you refused and made me wait."

"You disobeyed, you would not grow,
The walk of faith, you would not know,
So I got tired, I got fed up,
And there I dropped you on your butt."

"Because in life, there comes a time,
When one must fight, and one must climb,
When one must rise and take a stand,
Or leave their butt prints in the sand."[3]

Do you see how much you matter to God? God says, "Get over yourselves. You could be heroes." You could. It is possible. If God matters more to you than you matter to yourself, then yes, you could be heroes.

Fred Craddock tells a story about a young man in his early twenties dying of AIDS in an Atlanta hospital:

> He had no church connection, but someone said he had relatives who had been in the church, so they called the minister of that church, and the minister went to the hospital. The young man was almost dead, just gasping there, and the minister came to the hospital, stood out in the hall, and asked them to open the door. When they opened the door, he yelled in a prayer. Another minister there in south Atlanta heard about it and rushed to the

hospital, hoping that he was still alive. She got to the hospital, went in to the room, went over by the bed, and pulled the chair by the bed. This minister lifted his head and cradled it in her arm. She sang. She quoted scripture. She prayed. She sang. She quoted scripture. She prayed. And he died. Some of the seminarians said, "Weren't you scared? He had AIDS!" She said, "Of course I was scared. I bet you I bathed sixty times." "Well, then, why did you do it?" And she said, "I just imagined if Jesus had gotten the call, what he would've done. I had to go."[4]

Are you ready for prime time? It's some kind of spotlight, isn't it? The truth is, you're not in it. That's the idea. God is in the spotlight, not you. You're just in the shadows, in the wings, doing the heroic work that Christ has called you to.

You could be heroes. No—you are heroes, every one of you. You are here. And here, on this Sunday morning, you have said by your very presence, "God matters."

But here's the clincher. Tomorrow, will you make that same claim? At work, at home, on the Little League fields, on the northbound 405, at the market, on the riverbank? Will God matter then?

Tomorrow, you could be heroes. You could be. You will be.

ART GALLERY

Major Motion Picture Clips

Clip 1: *October Sky* (1999). In Coalwood, West Virginia, all the boys grow up to be coal miners and Homer Hickam has no reason to think he'll be any different. Too small to earn a football scholarship, Homer has no way out of his predetermined life—until the Soviet satellite Sputnik flies over the October sky and changes everything. It's 1957, and Homer's world just got a lot bigger. Though his father is mine superintendent and has no greater wish than to see his sons follow in his footsteps, Homer embarks on a mission to build and launch his own homemade rockets with the help of his loyal band of friends. Though their frequent mistakes nearly get them shut down, their successes inspire the whole town to believe that miracles can happen even in Coalwood and that there's nothing wrong with shooting for the stars.

When his father suggests that Homer should keep pursuing rocketry as a hobby, Homer tells his father that he's never going back to mining. *(VHS, 1:17:26–1:19:56) Total time: 2:30.*

Clip 2: *Rudy* (1993) is the true story of an ordinary kid who pours his heart and soul into playing for the Notre Dame football team. Overcoming tremendous odds, not the least of which is his small stature, Rudy realizes his dream and makes history.

In this scene, Rudy lands a position on the defensive practice squad and comes face-to-face with the physical brutality of a game he is too small to play. Repeatedly hit from every side by players twice his size, Rudy continues to rise to his feet for the sake of fulfilling his lifelong dream. *(VHS, 1:13:40–1:15:11) Total time: 1:31.*

"Man on the Street"

Interview people on the street, or people in your congregation, seeking responses to the following question:

> Name one dream that you've always wanted to fulfill but never had the time or fortune to pursue.

Pop Music

The Wallflowers, "Heroes"

While the guns are "shot above our heads, we kissed, as though nothing could fall." Love is the heroic deed, even if it lasts just for a day.

Bob Dylan, "You Gotta Serve Somebody"

This enduring classic reminds us that regardless of our petty titles and status, we all have to serve somebody...whether it's the devil or the Lord.

Poetry

Emily Dickinson, "492"

To offer brave assistance
To Lives that stand alone—
When One has failed to stop them—
Is Human—but Divine.[5]

Literature

Stephen Ambrose, *Undaunted Courage*

On his thirty-first birthday, [Meriwether] Lewis wrote, in a famous passage, "This day I completed my thirty-first year...I reflected that I had as yet done but little, very little indeed, to further the happiness of the human race, or to advance the information of the succeeding generation. I viewed with regret the many hours I have spent in indolence, and now soarly feel the want of that information which those hours would have given me had they been judiciously expended." He resolved: "In the future, to live for *mankind,* as I have heretofore lived for myself."[6]

Images

Historic legends and heroes, such as Martin Luther King, Jr., Babe Ruth, Mother Teresa, or Sojourner Truth.

Enough Is Enough

Exodus 20:15

You shall not steal. (Exodus 20:15)

So you're standing in line at Disneyland with your kids, wondering how in the world you're going to get out of this place without having to take out a line of credit. You're adding up the cotton candy, the four Astro Burger meals, the Goofy hats and matching sweatshirts, and the six dozen red ropes that you'll have to buy once you get through the gates, and you're beginning to get a bitter taste of reality in the sweet land of fantasy, right? Standing there in line, you glance over at the sign that displays the cost of admissions, and you begin to get a little creative. Kids are cheaper—that's good. Kids two and under are free—that's got some real possibilities, right? You begin to wonder if maybe your youngest kid might pass for two and under—it's entirely possible. *He's not two and under,* you think to yourself, *but he definitely has moments in which he acts like he's two and under, and that ought to count for something. Maybe the guy at the gate wouldn't notice. I should have brought the stroller today,* you say to yourself. *That would have been more convincing. He'd look more like a toddler if I had brought the stroller along.* But then you remember that you actually gave that stroller away after his *sixth* birthday. You look down at the little guy. He's clutching your hand, beaming a smile right at you. You're his hero. You're the next best thing to Ken Griffey, Jr. You, Junior, Pokemon, and maybe the Backstreet Boys—that's his whole world. You really think that you can pull this one off. What do you do?

A guy is selling big-screen TVs out of his unmarked moving van down at the local swap meet. These units retail for $2,000 over at TV Depot, but this guy's unloading them, brand new in the box for $499, and you think, *now that's a steal.* "Cash only," the sign reads. He calls you over to the truck, says he's got a real *hot* deal for you. You look down at your kid, who's still clutching your hand. You think about how heroic Griffey Jr. would look on one of these tubes. You've got the cash. What do you do?

Back at Disneyland a woman in front of you drops a load of cash on the ground. You don't actually *see* her drop it, but she's the nearest person to the small treasure. She's heading over to the candy cart to get those six dozen red ropes for her full-price kids. It's a tough call. *It could be hers, but it might not hers. Finders-keepers?* What do you do?

Or you finally go to buy those six dozen red ropes, but the woman at the candy cart only charges you for five dozen. She's made a mistake, doesn't know it. What do you do?

Or the cable company forgets to scramble all of your premium channels, and you're only paying for the basic package. Free Disney Channel, free Sports Center with Griffey Jr. What do you do?

Or you lose your wedding ring, so you file a claim with the insurance company. They pay you fair market value for your loss, which was more than reasonable. And now you won't believe it, but right after you cash that insurance check and go buy that big-screen TV, you find the ring. Actually, it was your neighbor who found it while cleaning out that old *stroller* you gave her. So there you are, sitting there eating red ropes, watching your free Griffey Jr. sports channel on your steal-of-a-deal big screen with your six-year-old who sometimes acts like he's two, and you wonder, only briefly, *what do I do?*

Not you, I'm sure, but someone perhaps like you, and me, since 52 percent of all working Americans admit to stealing stuff or skimming money from the company coffers or stretching time on the company clock. And somehow we're still able to act surprised that 30 percent of all American teenagers admit to stealing something from a store and that 25 percent of high school students admit to stealing grades by cheating. What's the world coming to, you ask? More is caught, says the proverb, than is taught, which means that the little child clutching your heroic hand will learn more from what you do than from what you say.

You shall not steal. It's another tough one to talk about, isn't it? It's right up there with the commandment prohibiting adultery, which, incidentally, is a particular form of theft. Sex and theft are often at the forefront of our cultural dialogue, yet we do not particularly enjoy hearing about them in church. We avoid talking about sex during church much like we avoid talking about church during sex; discussing the two in either context has a way of ruining the moment. Likewise, when we talk about theft in church, especially the kind of theft that you and I are prone to practice, we begin to see how the word of God has a way of cutting a little closer to the bone than we'd prefer, in areas of our life that we'd prefer to keep private.

The commandment tells us that we need to keep our hands off the stuff that's not ours to take. But it's difficult these days to discern what belongs to us and what belongs to our neighbors and what it means to acquire stuff wrongly. It's part of the American experience, isn't it? From the first day we stepped foot on this continent we've been taking someone's stuff. The Protestant work ethic and the spirit of capitalism, as Max Weber called it, has always had a way of nurturing our drive to acquire, to succeed, to get ahead, to prosper, to bend the rules, to rationalize and deceive by legally permissible means. How can we even know if the polls concerning stealing are even accurate, given the fact that most of us are unsure what constitutes stealing and what is merely a culturally acceptable way of self-advancement?

God understood our human proclivity for acquiring stuff deceitfully, so he gave us a commandment that tells the truth on us. God declared a prohibition on acquiring anything that is not ours by any unfair means. That means that if it hasn't been legitimately given to us, if we haven't inherited it, if we haven't paid fair price for it, if we haven't created it, if we haven't honestly earned it or traded for it, then it's not ours to take. The Disneyland deception, the red ropes, the big-screen TV, and all the rest seem to fall under this blanket coverage.

But more than that, the seventh commandment is a statement about the way we are to perceive other people. It's God's way of reminding us that people are not to be perceived as an opportunity for exploitation and self-advancement. God didn't create you to serve me, to help me get ahead at your expense. God created you to serve God, and our vocation as Christians is to work together in order to accomplish that creative purpose in this world. That's the Christian vision of the seventh commandment. It has a way of going beyond our own personal, private ethical dilemmas. It's a statement about how we are to live in community.

Every Sunday here we do a radical thing—many radical things, actually. First, we give some of our stuff away. It's called the offering around here. It's a reminder that if we believe that

God created us to serve God, then we've been given the means by which to do that together. My offering is added to your offering so that a portion of our stuff is held in common for God's work. That's the countercultural vision handed down to us by our ancestors in the book of Acts, who realized that one of the primary values of Christian communal life is sharing our resources for the common good (4:32–37). They remind us that when Christians get together, they share their stuff so that no one will have need, and when no one has need, God is glorified and served. Where else in the world do we freely put a portion of our stuff in a common pot and trust that it is the right thing to do? The Super Bowl pool at the office doesn't qualify.

Around here, that means I give so that my children and your children might come to know Jesus Christ and his saving grace in the Sunday school classrooms, in the youth programs, in the after-school programs. It means that I give so that we all can hear the band and the choir sing about Jesus and his saving grace. It means that I give so that somewhere in Africa, or downtown Los Angeles, or downtown Moscow, a portion of my gift might help our United Methodist missionaries tell the story about Jesus and his saving grace to someone who needs to hear it.

When I cling to my stuff and seek only to acquire more stuff, it's hard to love the one in Moscow or Los Angeles or in that Sunday school room or the ones in the chairs before me, because I see them merely as an impediment to my self-advancement. But something happens when I give some of it away. I can see their faces, see Jesus in their faces, and express my love for them and for God by serving them in tangible ways. They're no longer objects that serve no greater purpose than to help me get ahead. They are real. They are the body of Christ.

Most mainline Protestant church members give only 1 to 2 percent of their income to the church so that this kind of work can happen. Many mainline Protestant churches are also in serious decline. A curious correlation, don't you think? Jesus said, "Where your treasure is, there your heart will be also" (Mt. 6:21).

But we do another radical thing every Sunday. I hope you do it more than once a week. It's that line in the Lord's Prayer, the line that says, "Give us this day our daily bread." When you pray that prayer, you're asking that God would simply give you the very basics, give you only what is required for you to live another day, give you what is sufficient. Out in the desert the Israelites discovered that manna was all they could legitimately expect from God for their physical hunger. Daily bread. They didn't know from one day to the next where they'd get their next meal. But every morning, it fell from heaven, and every morning, it was enough.

When you discover that daily bread is enough in your life, you're cured from what many these days are calling *affluenza*. It's the sickness of our day. The drive to acquire, the quest for stuff, even at the expense of our neighbor. There's no inoculation for it, save for a simple prayer that reads, "Give us this day our daily bread." When we get it, and when we thank God for it, we're more apt to give it away than we are to hoard it or take it from someone else.

When author Anne Lamott found Jesus after a painful journey through addiction, she fell into a small African American church in Marin, California. She notes that it was the generosity of that church that saved her life. She was the only white person in the church. She was also pregnant, alone, and trying to find her way home.

> When I was at the end of my rope, the people at St. Andrew tied a knot in it for me and helped me hold on...Sam was welcomed and prayed for at St. Andrew seven months before he was born...And then almost immediately they set about providing for us. They brought clothes, they brought me casseroles to keep in the freezer, they brought me assurance that this baby was going to be a part of the family. They began slipping me money.
>
> Now, a number of the older black women live pretty close to the bone financially on small Social Security checks. But routinely they sidled up to me and stuffed bills in my pocket—tens and twenties. It was always done so stealthily that you might have thought they were slipping me bindles of cocaine. One of the most consistent donors was a very old woman named Mary Williams, who is in her mid-eighties now, so beautiful with her crushed hats and hallelujahs; she always brought me plastic Baggies full of dimes, noosed with little wire twists.[1]

A few years later, Anne Lamott hit it big with her first book, and several others followed. She believes that church saved her life. Even now, she still attends St. Andrew every Sunday, and

Mary Williams, she says, still brings her Baggies full of dimes. Now that Lamott doesn't need them, she gives them away to street people.

Daily bread. It *is* enough. The rest becomes bread for the world in the body of Christ. According to Jesus, it's the only way to squeeze through the eye of a needle without getting stuck.

ART GALLERY

Major Motion Picture Clips

Field of Dreams (1989) is the mythical story about a struggling Iowa farmer, Ray Kinsella (Kevin Costner), who obeys a mysterious voice in his cornfield that tells him to replace part of his crop with a baseball diamond, resulting in the magical meeting of baseball heroes from the past.

After Ray finishes building his field, Shoeless Joe Jackson (Ray Liotta) appears and preaches about the beauty of the game of baseball. This scene begins with Ray throwing batting practice to Shoeless Joe under the lights and ends with Shoeless Joe talking about how his love for the game was so great that he'd have played for nothing.

This scene captures the spirit of what it means to be in community and the immeasurable joy of giving back to the love that claims you. *(VHS, 21:35–25:54) Total time: 4:19.*

Pop Music

Supertramp, "Give a Little Bit"

The ageless tune that points to our "need to share," to "send a smile," to take the hand of "the man with the lonely eyes," and in so doing, to find ourselves and the way back home.

Collective Soul, "Collection of Goods"

Of all that we collect, it is the "peace, hope, words of care," and "love to share" that will "glamorize all of love's needs."

Alanis Morrisette, "Thank U"
A song of gratitude for all of life—"the silence, frailty, terror, disillusionment, providence, consequence," and "clarity" that grounds and unites us.

Images

Loaves of bread, churches, hands in an open, receptive posture.

Even Better than the Real Thing

Romans 13:8–14

Owe no one anything, except to love one another; for the one who loves another has fulfilled the law. (Romans 13:8)

So did you hear about this recent study that suggests that women use twice as many words as men do in a single day? I can tell already that some of you are not surprised by this. The study reveals that men, on average, use about fifteen thousand words per day; women, on the other hand, use close to thirty thousand words a day. That's absurd, isn't it? Thirty thousand words a day? How do you do that? Do you talk to yourself when no one's around? I asked Lori how this could be possible. She thought about it for a minute, and then said, "It's pretty clear to me. Women talk twice as much as men because we have to repeat everything we say." I said, "What's that?"

It's true. It's my confession to you. I'm not alone in this. And it's not just a male thing. It's cultural, even biological, perhaps. We suffer from selective hearing. We listen for, and hear, only what we want to hear, only what is useful to us, to our needs, to our wants. I wonder sometimes why I don't stop to listen more than I do; why I don't drop everything and shut up and listen to what the people around me are saying—saying not only with their words but with their very presence. But I already know why. The people who get me to stop and listen are the people who have something to give me, or the people to whom I owe something.

Isn't that the way the world works? In our culture, the person has been commodified—reduced to an object of value that can be bought or sold according to his or her usefulness to us. In the business world, we refer to people not as colleagues or friends, but contacts, right? We don't have lunch; we network. We don't help one another out; we invest in one's future. And we don't give anything away for free—a recommendation, a chance, a raise—without at least the unspoken understanding that one day we'll call back the favor when we need it. We don't even have to shake hands anymore. Instead, we pull out our little PDAs and beam each other all our vital stats. All acceptable in the business world; but what happens when it spills over into the personal, the spiritual, the communal?

I read recently in the *Wall Street Journal* about a church in Norfolk, Virginia, that holds debt liquidation revivals every month. Maybe you've heard about this. Mount Carmel Baptist Church has a mission: to get its members out of credit card debt. So far, fifty-six families in the church have been "delivered" from a total of $318,000 in debt. Once a month, everyone gets together on a Friday night for a revival. You drop in $300 each month, or whatever you can; the pastor picks a family or two; and just like that someone is delivered from credit card purgatory. The pastor has developed a plan so that everyone in the church will be free of credit card debt by the end of 2004. Apparently, this is what Jesus had in mind for the church. Lotto fever in the pews. Asked in a recent interview why he began this ministry, the pastor told the *Wall Street Journal,* "Because you can't serve your Master and Mastercard at the same time." Profound, isn't it? Is it the real thing, or is it just people using the church for self-gain, and a pastor using people just to fill the pews?

Maybe it's one of the harsh consequences of living in a capitalistic society, in which human relationships, spiritual matters, and the immeasurable, invaluable things of life are dealt like currency; maybe it's just human sinfulness and a sign of our deep estrangement from each other. There may be an infinite number of reasons for the many ways we use one another, but none of them make it justifiable. We love others in this culture of ours most often because they have something we want—money, status, sex, privilege, answers, potential, a way out, or a way in; and once we've acquired it, we consume it and toss what's left in the trash and move on. It makes the headlines and the evening news every day. From corporate malfeasance at Enron to sex scandals in Washington; from carjackings on Main Street to portfolio jackings on Wall Street—it's all the same. People using people, taking more than they give. Pump, dump, and run. And most of the time it's not only legal, but acceptable.

The apostle Paul is writing to the church in Rome—a church he's never been to. It's a pretty savvy church; the people are bright, educated, religious, experienced. If you can read the epistle to the Romans without giving yourself a brain cramp, you're doing better than most. It's a tough book—theologically thick, full of metaphysical labyrinths that are hard to navigate at times—hard, that is, until Paul gets to this little section we read from today, which reads more like an Ann Landers column than anything we're accustomed to from Paul.

He gives them some practical Christian advice. He says, "*Owe nothing to anyone* and you'll save yourself and the people in your life a lot of pain and grief." Within the context of this passage, Paul is saying that when you owe something to someone, you don't have a relationship with them—you have a deal; you are in the endless loop of give-and-take, the endless cycle of using and being used. You are an object, not a person. And you open yourself up to a whole grab bag of sins when you do that. Theft, killing, coveting, adultery—these in particular, says Paul, are the consequences of perceiving people as objects of measurable value rather than people of immeasurable worth.

Karl Barth noted that "love of another ought to be undertaken as the protest against the course of this world." Jesus undertook such a protest, using the single force of love to invert the cultural, religious distinctions between the haves and the have-nots, the clean and the unclean, the living and the socially dead, the found and the lost. And he proved that subversive love is the purest form of love because it is the love given freely to someone who is unable to repay it. It is love to the less-than-worthy, the less-than-us, making them more than they are and more than they could ever be without it, love that requires more than the world is apt to want to give because there is nothing to gain in the giving, save the quiet revelation that it is what the Father requires of those he loves. It is love that makes repayment an impossibility.

There is a reason why the poor are always with us, why three million kids in America go to school hungry, why the infirmed elderly die abandoned and alone in nursing homes we will never see, why 25 percent of the population living on the African continent suffer from AIDS while First World nations withhold stockpiles of effective medications. The reason, of course, is that they seemingly have nothing to give us for our love of them; there is no return on our investment.

I read the story recently of a boss who said to his employee, "Your shift is over; it's time for you to go home, I'm here to take your place." Strange words from a boss. But this was no ordinary changing of the guard on the factory floor. The boss was Alberta businessman Norbert Reinhart. The employee was Ed Leonard, of Creston, British Columbia, who had been on the job at a gold exploration site in Colombia when guerrillas took him hostage for ransom on June 24, 1997.

Rebel troops finance their war against the government by kidnapping prominent citizens and holding them for ransom. In 1997, there were more than 1,800 kidnapping cases in Colombia. Many kidnapping victims are never fully informed about the dangers of working in Colombia. Ed Leonard was one of the misinformed.

For 105 days, Leonard was held in various camps in the Andes Mountains. But on October 6, 1998, Ed Leonard came home. It happened because when all other efforts had failed to free him, Ed's boss, Norbert Reinhart, offered himself as a hostage in Ed's place. Months later, Reinhart was released after a ransom was paid.

"Greater love," says Jesus, "has no man than this—to lay down his life for his friends." And then he transcended even that great love for something still more excellent. He laid down his life for his enemies. "What good is it to you," he said, "if you love those who can repay you? I say, 'love your enemies,' for in doing so you will receive your reward in heaven."

I don't know how you get there, how you get to that point in your life, unless you've understood and experienced the depth of God's love in your own life, for you, when you have been less worthy and deserving of it, when you've recognized that there is no way to repay to debt, the ransom. It's something that can be preached, but until it is experienced, it is lifeless. I've seen it. But it's rare.

He reached the end of his rope. He threw himself over the edge one day, over the treacherous, lonely canyon of marital infidelity. Stayed out there for seven years. Didn't know how to pull himself up out of it, and was too afraid to ask for help. One day he finally lost his grip and nearly fell off the face of the earth. Lost contact with his family, his friends, his church. Lost everything, and he knew then that he'd have to go to the ends of the earth to get it back. He asked me how he could do this, and I told him that I knew of only one way—to ask for it. Grace is free, I told him, but it's not cheap. He couldn't buy it, earn it, or deal for it. It would be free, but it would come at an immeasurable cost for his family.

It took time. He stood at the door and knocked for a long time. It looked bleak. But eventually, they let him in, gave him a place to start over, a place in the very family he once destroyed.

Some people thought his wife and children were fools. Some thought the man didn't deserve it. Some thought he got off too easy. But a few understood. They understood that it wasn't about winners or losers, or fairness, or retribution. It was about the love of Jesus, which overcomes the world.

I want you to make it your mission this week to love someone who cannot repay you, because if they can repay you, there is at least some small hint that your love is an expression of your own selfish desire to get something in return. I want you to attempt to love purely this week, the way Jesus loves us—not according to our merits or worthiness, but according to our need. Love in such a way that you see, in the face of the loved, your own reflection, your own likeness, undone, undressed, unworthy.

I saw my own this week in the face of Thomas, who calls on me from time to time whenever he's in town. Thomas has been on the go for six years. He has the wild eyes of defenseless prey at dusk, with the sour smell of no home and a dark, wizened face that bears the map to his well-traveled soul. His six-and-a-half teeth keep his tongue from spilling out onto the floor when he speaks, and his purple cap rides high and graceful on his head, like a crown.

Thomas uses me—I feed him or give him grocery money. Likewise, I use Thomas—he's my therapist, my spiritual director. Thomas knows my trade; he built seven churches in downtown Detroit, served them all at the same time as a pastor. But now, as he tells people, he's a cathedral in the city, a pastor to the street people. Home is not where you come from, he tells me, but where you belong; and your legacy is not what you're doing, but who you are loving.

Thomas does love in the streets to the unloved, and every so often, he does love to the unloved in the suburbs, when they'll let him in. He came this week on the Metro to tell me he is proud of me and to ask me for a meal and a blessing. I consent.

I give him what I have and then lay a hand on his head as he lays a hand on my shoulder. *The Lord watch between me and thee*—offering gratitude for my friend, my pastor, this houseless saint.

And at the end of the day, when I go home after a long day of doing, I can still smell his hand on my shoulder—the smell of unrequited love.

ART GALLERY

Major Motion Picture Clips

Unstrung Heroes (1995) is a touching childhood memoir of Franz Lidz, a young Jewish boy who comes to depend on his two absurdly quirky uncles for comic relief and life lessons while dealing with his mother's grave illness.

In this recommended scene, Franz joins his eccentric uncle in search of lost things in the city. As his uncle rescues lost balls from the city's gutters, he tells Franz that he "can hear the sounds of the children who played with them." *(VHS 52:48–54:52) Total time: 2:20.*

Pop Music

Mary-Chapin Carpenter/Don Schlitz, "I Take My Chances"

The lonely narrator sits in a dark room and watches a television preacher offer salvation in return for a personal check. Disgusted and bored, the narrator flips the channel to CNN and lights another cigarette, confessing, *"I'll take my chances, forgiveness doesn't come with a debt."*

Images

Coca-Cola bottle (the supposed "real thing").

Divine Interruptions

Matthew 9:9–13, 18–26

While he was saying these things to them, suddenly a leader of the synagogue came in and knelt before him, saying, "My daughter has just died; but come and lay your hand on her, and she will live." And Jesus got up and followed him, with his disciples. (Matthew 9:18–19)

Both of my kids had birthdays this past week. It's a humbling moment, isn't it—watching your children turn the page on another calendar year, witnessing their gradual, inevitable progression toward that peculiar designation of *grown-up*? Alyson, now nine, is halfway there; Casey, a third of the way there. When you're a kid, you can't wait to get there, right? And when you get there, you wonder what all the hype was about, don't you? When you're a kid, your life is one long succession of interruptions and distractions. You bounce from one thing to another; adventure is king; novelty and wonder and enchantment are the lures that lead you along. The sight of a spider weaving a web in a woodpile stops you in your tracks; a rainbow captures your imagination; a mud puddle is something you walk through, not around; and a summer rain shower is something you drop everything for, if only to stand under it with your head raised and mouth wide open and arms outstretched—something you breathe in, taste, smell, hear, and touch.

So what happened? Somewhere along the way the spider becomes a pest, the rainbow a mere scientific phenomenon, the mud puddle a mess to avoid, the summer rain the ruin of a freshly waxed car.

For adults there is something comforting about our routines, our predictable plans, our schedules. Interruptions and distractions, we are told, are things to be avoided. How many seminars on *time management* have we attended in which we are told to eliminate the interruptions of our lives, to prioritize and categorize our time and tasks in order to more efficiently accomplish our personal goals? What was your first purchase out of college, once you landed that first job? A Day-Timer®, right? A PDA, perhaps. So you can manage your time, stay focused, keep on task, avoid distractions.

But while there is comfort in our routines and plans, there is something equally disenchanting about them. Growing up too often means giving up the mystery and wonder of our lives. Supertramp sang about that loss twenty-three years ago.

In their hit song "The Logical Song," they recall the wonder of childhood and the everyday miracles of life, when it seemed that all of nature was replete with awe and playfulness. But growing up means leaving all that behind for a logical, practical, sensible, enlightened life that, at the end of the day, creates a state of absurdity in which one's self-identity grows increasingly clouded and confused. After learning all there is to know, one question still remains—*"please tell me who I am."*

Who am I? Who are you? Are we the sum of all our work, all our knowledge, all our plans and routines? Are we captives to the urgency of our lives, held hostage to the clock, to our goals, to the immediacy of the now? Or are we more than that? When all the world's asleep, when finally you hit the pause button after running in fast-forward all day, and you begin, if only for a moment, to let the questions run deep. Who am I?

This passage from Matthew has Jesus running in fast-forward. Jesus has just entered his hometown, and the whole community is buzzing. Everyone has questions for him; everyone has something they need from him. Mostly, they just want to know what he knows, what he thinks, what he believes. "How can you say this, but do that? Why do you hang out with tax collectors and sinners? Why don't you and your disciples fast?" They've got all kinds of religious questions for Jesus; that's what religious people do, right? They have meetings. They debate over the right answers; they talk about religious matters. It's all so serious, so terribly boring. A bunch of religious people having another meeting to set things straight.

Jesus is stuck in the middle of it. He's in his hometown, after all. He's got to be nice, play fair, show respect. But as the meeting drags on and on, there is a sudden interruption—a leader of the synagogue pokes his head in and pulls Jesus out of the meeting. He says, "My daughter has just died, but come lay your hands on her, and she will live."

He slips through the door while the debate inside continues. And as he heads to the man's house, another interruption occurs. A woman who's been hemorrhaging for twelve years reaches out and grabs his robe, believing that if only she could touch even the very fringe of his robe she would be healed of her illness. She does. Jesus pauses to tell her, "Your faith has made you well." And it has; she is healed.

Jesus continues on, reaches the man's house, and quiets the flute players, telling them the girl is not dead. The crowds laugh; the girl *is* dead, they say, dead as dead can be. It's over, too late; let's get on with the funeral plans. But Jesus goes in, takes her by the hand, and the little girl comes out the front door on her rollerblades.

When Jesus turns around to leave, to get back to the meeting—a meeting, any meeting, because it's inevitable that someone will pull him into another meeting, another interruption, right?—he finds two blind men, crying out for mercy, begging for sight. He touches their eyes, and they are healed.

The passage begins with religious debate and controversy over belief, with meetings that Jesus appears to have had little passion or tolerance for; and it concludes with Jesus' touching people, healing people, which is his life purpose, his life mission. When you read the passage straight through, you wonder if Jesus was ever really able to accomplish anything he set out to do; every time he turns around, someone is interrupting him, pulling him aside, asking him for something only he can give them.

You ever feel like that? Ever had one of those days when you list all the things you must get done, only to have interruption after interruption, so that by the end of the day you have nothing tangible, measurable, to show for how you spent your time? We live in a culture that values *leafage* more than *rootage*. We look for fruit, for signs of progress, for results. So when someone interrupts us, when someone breaks into the progression of our plans, it becomes an inconvenience.

Jesus reminds us that it is the interruptions of our lives that are our life's work. Life is what happens when we're busy making plans, right? Real life, the real stuff of life, the marrow that feeds us, is not always in our work, but also in the pauses, the interruptions, the breaks, the gaps in our time.

But what do we say? "Hold on a moment. Just a minute. I'll be right there. I'll get to that someday." I know I find myself saying that to my kids more often than I wish; to my wife, my friends, my God—far more than I'd care to admit. "Just a minute." We end up living in the land of *someday*... "Someday I'm going to write that letter, make that call, rotate those tires."

Somewhere between all the demands the world places on us and all the things we love to do—somewhere between those two pulls, those two poles—is a God-infused moment of opportunity and grace, if we can bear to face it. To find it, we may have to reach beyond our Enlightenment minds, which have been trained to view the world critically, rationally; trained to break it down into small, measurable pieces in order to examine its parts, like an engine of an automobile. That's Enlightenment science for you, and we are children of the Enlightenment. If it can't be measured, it can't be real, can't be trusted. Just stick with the facts, stay on track. But there is something happening out there beyond the bare facts, something untracked, out on the margins, that bears a closer look.

I am a reader. I read not only because I love reading but also because I love books. My books are my tools; like a mechanic's toolbox, my bookshelves hold the instruments of my work. And more than reading a book once, I love going back and reading it twice—not for what the author wrote, but for what I wrote in the margins when I first read it. There is something out there in the margins that tells me more about myself than anything else—these little interruptions, little interludes, little flashes that speak to me, speak about me.

Take a hard look at your life. Look at all the work you do; look at all the demands people place on you; look at all your plans, all your goals, all your routines. And ask yourself, how much margin have I left in my life? How much space have I left for God to write his notes on the pages of my life, to interrupt my life and pull me out of where I am to where he is going in the world?

One late winter afternoon Frederick Buechner recalls that he was walking to a class he had to teach when he noticed the beginnings of what promised to be one of the great local sunsets—with all the right clouds and burning sky and dark trees on the horizon. He arrived at the classroom to find all the lights on and all the students chattering, and just as he was about to start the class, he felt the sudden impulse to snap off the lights, without warning. When he did, everything in the room disappeared save the burning sunset spilling through the west-facing window, and a sudden silence fell across the room as the students and their teacher watched for twenty minutes while the extraordinary spectacle faded slowly away. He writes:

> For over twenty minutes nobody spoke a word. Nobody said anything. We just sat there in the near-dark and watched one day of our lives come to an end...What was great was the un-busyness of it. It was taking unlabelled, un-allotted time just to look with maybe more than our eyes at what was wonderfully there to be looked at without any obligation to think any constructive thoughts about it or turn it to any useful purpose later, without any weapon at hand in the dark to kill the time it took...The way this world works, people are very apt to use the words they speak not so much as way of revealing, but as a way of concealing who they really are and what they really think, and that is why more than a few moments of silence with people we do not know well are apt to make us so tense and uneasy. Stripped of our verbal camouflage, we feel unarmed against the world and vulnerable, so we start babbling about anything just to keep the silence at bay. But if we can bear to let it be, silence, of course, can be communion at a very deep level indeed, and that half hour of silence was just that, and perhaps that was the greatest part of it all.[1]

Buechner understood what Jesus most fully embodied and what every Christian struggles daily to put into practice: that there are moments to *cause,* and moments to *pause;* moments in which we must work to make a difference in the world, and moments in which we must pause to consider what kind of difference we are making, if any at all. I do not know how you separate the two, or even know the difference between them, because more often than not both moments are upon us simultaneously, as they were for Jesus. All I know is that he was able to make the inconvenient interruptions of his life count for something more than the expediency the world so highly valued, and values still. Which, perhaps, proved to be his most productive work of all: not merely making a difference in the world, but making a different world altogether—where the dead are not merely mourned but raised; where the blind are not only touched but also given sight; where the sick are not only comforted but also healed.

Jesus made time for both kinds of moments in his life, no doubt about it. But one of them seemed to matter more to him than the other. And if you're still unsure of which it was, I get the feeling that, if you took the time to ask him, he'd take the time to tell you.

ART GALLERY

Major Motion Picture Clips

Grand Canyon (1991) is an introspective tale of the unlikely friendship of two men from different worlds brought together when one (Kevin Kline) finds himself in danger in the other's (Danny Glover) violent neighborhood. Other characters from contrasting Los Angeles origins (including Steve Martin, Alfre Woodard, and Mary-Louise Parker) also cross paths in this soul-searching lament of modern social conflicts and the spiritual numbness/callousness of modern humanity.

After Mack (Kline) is rescued by a stranger, Simon (Glover), from an attempted robbery/assault in the streets of the inner city late one evening, he begins to awaken to the growing sense of having been the beneficiary of providence—not just in this most recent experience, but years earlier, too, when he is pulled from the curb by a stranger and his life is spared from certain death on Miracle Mile. Although he never had the opportunity to thank that stranger—a woman wearing a Pittsburgh Pirates hat (Mack's favorite team)—he wonders, "was she real, or sent from somewhere else?" In this scene, mindful of the divine interruptions of his life, he resolves to thank Simon for his kindness and open the door to something more—"I didn't want you to just disappear." *(VHS, 1:12:10–1:14:30) Total time: 2:20.*

Pop Music

Sheryl Crow, "Soak Up the Sun"
"It's not having what you want/It's wanting what you've got."

Jennifer Knapp, "Visions"
"The world is my Jordan, someday I'm gonna cross..."

Images

Clocks, calendars, day-planners, and personal digital assistants (PDAs).

No Bull

Exodus 32:1–14

He took the gold from them, formed it into a mold, and cast an image of a calf; and they said, "These are your gods, O Israel, who brought you up out of the land of Egypt!" (Exodus 32:4)

I saw a television infomercial advertising this new, revolutionary diet drink on the market that's supposed to burn fat while you sleep. Have you heard about this? Apparently, it really works. Two hours before you hit the sack you just drop a few scoops of this magic powder into a glass, add eight ounces of water, stir it up, and suck it down. You wake up the next morning looking like Ally McBeal. It actually burns the fat while you sleep. No more yoga; no more Lifecycle at the gym; no more Jenny Craig microwavable meals. Just to prove their point, they show you all these "before" and "after" pictures of the miserable and the beautiful, right? Why? Because seeing is believing. Go to bed looking like Free Willy and wake up looking like a greyhound. We'll believe just about anything, won't we?

A man knocked on my door a few weeks ago peddling his magical stain remover. Has he been to your home yet? He takes out his Sharpie pen, writes his name on his denim pant leg, pours a little stain remover over it, and wipes away the ink. A Sharpie pen's ink, for heaven's sake—disappearing right before my eyes. Lori says to me, "Think about it, for just $39.99, you can finally get all those Sharpie pen stains out of your jeans." I'm wondering when Sharpie pen stains became a cultural epidemic. Did I miss something? But it was pretty incredible, that stuff. We'll believe just about anything, won't we?

All that unsightly back hair you have—there's a product for that. All those facial blemishes from your adolescence—you can wipe them all away. Your third-grader is flunking math—we've got a tutor in a milk shake for that. If you spend enough time watching late-night television, you'll start to believe just about anything, right?

But it's not just television. Seeing is believing in our culture. I read about Gerald Barnes recently. Did you hear about this guy? For twenty-five years, Gerald Barnes fooled the medical world into believing he was a doctor. He came from Chicago, after losing his pharmacist's license for defrauding the Medicaid system, and—without any training in the medical profession—took up clinical practice near Hollywood, where his acting abilities made him a star. Using copies of a medical license and medical degree belonging to a real physician by the same name, Barnes was later recruited by an Irvine clinic and, for twenty-five years, treated thirty to forty patients a day—suturing wounds, reading X-rays, interpreting lab results, diagnosing and misdiagnosing major illnesses. He even contracted with the U.S. government to perform physicals on, of all people, FBI agents. You know what they said after they caught "Dr." Barnes? They said, "When people see someone wearing a white medical jacket and see the credentials hanging on the wall, they'll believe just about anything."

When we need a little assurance, when we need something to believe in, we all go looking for a little eye candy, don't we? The Israelites did.

We make a big deal about this story from Exodus. A golden calf, idol worship, God's chosen ones choosing a cheap alternative to the real thing. It's such an ironic story, given the fact that Moses, just a few chapters earlier, laid down the law—the Ten Commandments—for the Israelites. It's ironic because, as you'll recall, the first of the commandments said, "You shall have no other gods before me." And the second, "You shall not make any graven images of me." In other words, depend on me and me alone. No one else, no cheap imitations, no caricatures. I am enough.

So Moses lays it out for them and then heads up Mount Sinai, leaving Aaron in charge of the six hundred thousand Israelites. Moses climbs up the mountain, camps out for forty days and forty nights, getting instructions from the Lord on how to build the tabernacle, how to ordain priests, how to run a capital funds campaign and balance a budget. It's like seminary in forty days for Moses, a six-week boot camp with God. There's no guitar strumming "Kum ba Yah" up there; it's all work—exhausting, mind-bending, hard work. Moses is going to come down that mountain with Israel's future in his hands.

Meanwhile, the inmates are running the asylum down at the foot of the mountain. They're getting restless, right? Forty days without Moses is starting to feel like forty years for the Israelites. They've been in the desert too long; their feet are blistered and tired; their necks are stiff; they're sick of eating manna three times a day; they want to get home, get to the promised land. They're impatient. They can't wait. "We have no idea what happened to Moses," they say. "But Aaron, it's time to pack it in and get moving."

Without Moses, the Israelites couldn't tell you much about God. Moses was their source, their intermediary, their authority on God. These Israelites had never encountered God personally; had never heard from God, touched God, or talked to him. Moses did all that for them. But Moses was gone; and for all they know, he may never come back.

So they tell Aaron, "Throw something together for us that will stand for God, something that can go before us to lead the way, something we can see, so that we can believe in something to get us home. It doesn't matter what it looks like. How about something in gold—something shiny?

Now, I just don't know what Aaron was thinking. Somehow Aaron thought a cow would be inspiring. Maybe it had something to do with the cow being a familiar cultic symbol of fertility; maybe Aaron was just hungry—it could have been a seven-layer burrito, for that matter. But they all brought Aaron their gold—their best, which happened to belong to the Egyptians before they got out of Dodge and escaped slavery—and Aaron melted it down, came up with a cow, of all things, and said to the people, "Take a look at this. Now, this is something to believe in, something to hang your hat on. A cow." And they all cried out, "Holy cow!" And they danced, because they had something—a cow—they could believe in.

I wish I could laugh, but I know I'm not much different when it comes to wanting something to believe in. When you lose touch with God—when you can no longer see him, feel him, or hear him—you start to look for something more tangible that might represent him—something that represents his goodness, his blessing in your life, his promise. It's not so much that they wanted *another* god; they weren't looking to worship an *idol* any more than you and I set out to worship the idols of our day. They just wanted something to symbolize the one God they thought they knew, the God who led them out of Egypt and promised to take them home. They just wanted something they could see, because seeing is believing.

We do that. We take our experience of God and melt it down into something that will get us where we want to go, something that fits our lifestyle, our needs, our cultural priorities. And we call it God.

You could say that "family values" has become a sort of god for many North American Christians. Not at all a bad thing, family values. It's biblical—you can't deny that. And in an election year, it has a rather compelling political ring to it. Take care of your nuclear family; stay committed in your conventional marriage; assume your biblical family role; go to church. It is a godly thing to do. But I'll tell you, it's not God. It's not something to *believe* in. "Whoever loves father and mother more than me," says Jesus, "is not worthy of me; and whoever loves son or daughter more than me is not worthy of me" (Mt. 10:37).

Or take prosperity, which is another golden calf for many Christians. There's a lot of that kind of preaching. Work hard; earn an honest wage; work your way up, and get rewarded for your efforts. Be faithful; follow God's rules; get wealthy. The prosperous life looks a lot like a blessing, providence, destiny. Maybe. Maybe not. Prosperity is not something to believe in. The rain falls on the just and the unjust. Blessed are the poor, the have-nots, said Jesus. Seeing is not believing.

Or take the megachurch fascination—this can be a golden calf for some preachers. I talk to some of them, talk to preachers who go to these conferences to chase after the next big thing, to learn how it's done, to *become* the next big thing. "Just look at all those people they draw," they say. "The buildings, the people, the money. They must be doing something right over there." Maybe. There's a very good chance they are—I don't doubt that. But maybe not. Seeing is not believing. Size is not something to believe in. "For where two or three are gathered in my name," says Jesus, "I am there among them" (Mt. 18:20). Now that's something to believe in.

We all have our sacred cows—prejudices, political ideologies, religious dogmas, possessions, opinions, lifestyles. We all take what we know of God and melt it down into something more reasonable, something more manageable, something more tangible. And we put it before us and follow it, thinking we're heading for home, heading for the promised land. Meanwhile, God is still up there on the mountain—the *real thing* is still up there drawing up a road map that we can't even read because we're too busy packing our bags in pursuit of our sacred cows, our cheap imitations. We're like the blind men feeling out the elephant—some of us are touching the trunk; some of us are holding on to the tail; and we all start to believe that what we can touch, what we can see, is the whole thing, the real thing.

But Moses preached a radical monotheism—an uncompromising, far-reaching belief in the one and only God who is larger than life itself; a God who cannot be reduced or divided or captured in a symbol or an agenda or a fad, no matter how good or right or godly it may appear to be. Throughout the entire experience of the Israelites in the wilderness, from the day they fled slavery in Egypt and marched straight into the sea to the very moment they camped out at the foot of Mount Sinai and waited for Moses to come down the mountain, the Israelites had to trust in a God they could not see or touch; up until then, only Moses was given to experience that personal, direct relationship with God. The people had to depend on Moses to deliver the goods. They had to get used to an invisible God; they had to trust and believe in what they could not see.

I'm not sure it's much different for you and me. If seeing God is believing in God, most of us, at the end of the day, don't have a whole lot to hang our hats on. Between the evening news and the morning headlines, between the wars we wage internationally and the wars we wage in our own homes and relationships, it's hard to see God in everything that's wrong in the world. "Blessed are those," says Jesus, "who have not seen and yet...believe" (Jn. 20:29).

God is up to something in the Exodus story, and he's up to something in our world. He's drawing boundaries between heaven and earth so that we don't confuse his power and identity and promise with something as cheap as a cow, or a car, or a job, or six-pack abs, or anything else we are apt to want to worship in this world. He's choosing to remain hidden so that we will learn to live by faith and obedience and not by sight and independence. He's choosing to remain nameless—what does Moses say to God? "What do I tell them if they ask me your name, if they want a name before they agree to follow you?" And God says, "Tell them my name is 'I AM,' tell them that I am who I am." God remains nameless so that we won't stick his good name on everything we like in this world, everything that looks good and feels good. God is up to something here. God is working under the assumption that we will either follow him on his terms, and he will reveal himself to us when the time is right, when we are ready; or we will melt down what we know of him and follow that. But God knows there is only one way out of the wilderness. We can either graze in the fields of our sacred cows, living by sight, or we follow him with the eyes of faith to the promised land—a place that has to be believed before it can be seen.

Now, I know that's a hard sell these days. I know that a lot of preaching seeks to clarify and make sense of what we struggle to understand, to make rational what is transcendent. But what if, in our worship and our preaching, we leave enough room for God to work in the mystery of what cannot be seen or explained? What if, instead of believing in what we see, which is often only what we choose to see anyway, we believe in what God reveals to us in our experience, which more often than not eludes even our best attempts to explain it? I think of the two disciples, after the resurrection, who are walking on the road to Emmaus when the risen, disguised Jesus joins them and they do not know it, who later say, "Did not our hearts burn when he walked with us?" I think of the blind man who is given sight by Jesus, who later tells his friends, "I don't know what happened; all I know is that I was blind but now I see." I think of so many of you who tell me from time to time, I can't explain it; I don't know what exactly is happening in my life. But I can feel Him; I can sense that God is up to something."

I want you to know that that is enough to keep you at the foot of the mountain, waiting for God to reveal more of himself. For today, that mystery, that experience is enough. Tomorrow, it may be different; tomorrow, if you don't sell out to other gods, it will be different. Don't melt it down today into something you can control, something you can manage, something you can worship tomorrow. Look behind it, to the One who gives it, the One who will give it again and again in fresh, new ways. The Lord is the same yesterday and today and tomorrow, says scripture; but it also says the Lord is new every morning.

I have to work at that in my life. I start to think I understand the way God works. My theology becomes a sacred cow. Whatever doesn't fit comfortably within that framework, I too easily dismiss. Mystery becomes an inconvenience. I live by sight.

Wednesday night I received a phone call from a woman in crisis. She says she's worshiped here before but moved to an apartment in Dana Point earlier this year. She's forty-two years old, a single mom to a fifteen-year-old daughter and an eighteen-year-old autistic daughter. She tells me she is dying of ovarian cancer and just came home from the hospital after her last round of chemotherapy. "No more chemo," she says. "I want to spend whatever time I have with my kids." Someone from a hospice had just left after giving her a morphine injection. She's two months behind in her rent. Her car was impounded. A collection agency is planning to take her furniture. Her disability check hasn't yet arrived and won't for another six weeks. She needs help.

I get all kinds of calls from people in financial crisis. Not all of them are legitimate. In fact, many of them are motivated by drug and alcohol addictions, and I have to dig around more than I would like in order to weed out the real cries for help from the desperate cries for a fix. It's not easy doing that. After a while, it's hard not to be skeptical whenever the phone rings. My sacred cow starts mooing when I hear some of these stories. Seeing is believing, and I know a dying person when I see one.

So I told Peggy that I'd need to see her in order to assess her needs before doing anything for her. She invited me to her apartment, and I took Dave Scharp with me—one of our members, a physician and a member of our Mile Twenty pastoral care team—figuring that between the two of us, we could get to the truth.

It didn't take long to get to the truth. The bathrobe and the scarf covering her hairless scalp were the first clues. The canker sores in her mouth and throat, the side effects of chemotherapy, were not props. We talked; I asked questions—maybe too many questions—until it occurred to me that a woman with a terminal illness doesn't have much time for a trivial interrogation. After ten minutes, my skepticism turned into compassion, and I realized that God was up to something in that moment—something mysterious, something I couldn't dismiss. I thought to myself, *of all the places I could be right now, how did I end up here, in this apartment, on this night, with this stranger? This wasn't on my calendar, wasn't in my plans.* But this God of mine had been up on the mountain, drawing up a road map for the day, and in my haste to move on and in my pursuit of a cheap imitation of the real thing, I almost missed it. Almost. Until it occurred to me that God was in that place, and in meeting him, how could I not give him what he required—my worship, my reverence, my gold?

The grace, of course, is that God does come down the mountain, for the Israelites and for us. For the Israelites, he came down through the person of Moses, whose mission was to make God real among them. For you and me, he came down in the person of Jesus, the Son of God, the God-with-us who, like Moses, pleads with God not to destroy us on the spot but to give us a second chance, to have mercy on those who dance even still around their golden calves while the real thing hangs on a tree. "Father, forgive them, for they do not know what they are doing."

And somehow all the pleading works. God relents, gives us a second chance. I don't know why. That's a mystery I cannot explain. I just believe he does. I don't believe *everything* I see. But I do believe that.

ART GALLERY

Major Motion Picture Clips

Dogma (2000) is a highly irreverent film about two fallen angels, Loki and Bartleby, attempting to jerry-rig the entire cosmological system and gain entrance into heaven through a loophole in church law. The heroine of the film, Bethany, is commissioned by a heralding angel to intervene and save humanity, despite her doubts and spiritual angst. Bethany's mission sets her off on an extraordinary journey of mystery, comedy, and suspense as she meets up with heaven-sent messengers, a two-thousand-year-old "apostle" with an attitude, a petulant demon, a heavenly muse, and two cheeky prophets named Jay and Silent Bob.

The recommended scene finds Cardinal Glick (George Carlin) introducing the new church marketing campaign, "Catholicism Wow," on the steps of the New Jersey Cathedral. As a substitute for the outdated crucifix, which gives people "the willies," Cardinal Glick unveils "Buddy Christ"—a "booster" icon closely resembling the familiar "Bob's Big Boy" effigy. *(VHS, 0:02:14–0:03:50) Total time: 1:36.*

Prayer

Thomas Merton (1915–68), "A Prayer"

My Lord God
I have no idea where I am going.
I do not even see the road ahead of me.
I cannot know for certain where it will end.
Nor do I really know myself,
and the fact that I think I am following
your will does not mean
that I am actually doing so.
But I believe that my desire to please you
does in fact please you.
And I hope that I have that desire
in all that I am doing.
I hope that I will never do anything
apart from that desire.
And I know that if I do this
you will lead me by the right road
though I may know nothing about it.
Therefore will I trust you always
though I may seem to be lost
and in the shadow of death
I will not fear,
for you are ever with me
and you will never leave me
to face my perils alone.[1]

Images

Emil Nolde, *Dance around the Golden Calf* (1910). Oil on canvas. View this and other art images at www.artchive.com.

The Truth Is Out There

Mark 16:1–15

"He has been raised; he is not here." (Mark 16:6b)

One of my favorite writers, Annie Dillard, tells of a particular experience she had growing up in the suburbs of Pittsburgh during the 1950s. Dillard was seven years old at the time, and it happened that one winter morning six inches of snow had fallen on her neighborhood. She found herself with a group of neighborhood boys, standing in a front yard along a well-trafficked street, making fresh snowballs and taking aim at each car that happened to pass by.

A black Buick slowly made its way down the street that morning, and the group quickly spread out, waited for the right moment, and fired away. "A soft, fresh snowball hit the driver's windshield right before the driver's face. It made a smashed star with a hump in the middle." It wasn't unusual for them to hit their target, but this time, much to their surprise, the car pulled over and stopped. "Its wide black door opened; a man got out of it, running." As Dillard says, "He didn't even stop to close the car door."

> He ran after us and we ran away from him...He was in city clothes: a suit and tie, street shoes. Any normal adult would have quit...But this man was gaining on us. All of a sudden we were running for our lives. Wordless, we split up...everyone for himself. And everyone had vanished except Mikey Fahey. Poor Mikey, I trailed him. And the driver of the Buick sensibly picked the two of us to follow. The man apparently had all day.
>
> He chased us around the yellow house and up a backyard path...under a low tree, up a bank, through a hedge, down some snowy steps, and across the grocery

> store's driveway...through backyards and porches and over woodpiles; he kept coming. He chased us silently, block after block, over picket fences, through thorny hedges, between houses, around garbage cans and across streets. Every time I glanced back, I expected he would have quit...[but] this ordinary adult evidently knew what I thought only children...knew: that you have to fling yourself at what you're doing, you have to point yourself, forget yourself, aim, dive.
>
> He chased us through the backyard labyrinths of ten blocks before he caught us by our jackets. He caught us and we all stopped. We all stood staggering, half-blinded, coughing, in an obscure hilltop backyard: a man in his twenties, a boy, a girl...The chewing out was redundant, a mere formality, and beside the point. The point was that he had chased us passionately without giving up, and so he had caught us—this sainted, skinny furious redheaded man who wished to have a word with us.[1]

Having grown up Catholic, I had always imagined when I was a child that God was sort of like the man in the black Buick who was easily provoked, the kind of God who, if you crossed him, would chase you ten blocks through snow if he had to, just to make his point. And he would catch you, sooner or later. He'd keep you in line, keep you on your toes, so that sooner or later you'd drop the snowballs and grow up and maybe even join the priesthood. I had always figured that the only time God would get involved in my life was when I had done something wrong; so that as long as I wasn't lobbing snowballs at his big black Buick, he'd just keep driving by, and everything would be just fine. But if the Buick came to a stop and the big door opened, then the chase was on.

You don't have to grow up Catholic to think that way. We all, to some degree, have this inherent fear of getting too close to God. When something goes wrong in our lives, the first question we often ask ourselves is, "What did I do? Is this disappointment, this tragedy, this failure a sign that God has finally caught me, and now I've got to pay for my past?" We've all asked that question before.

But every year, at Easter, we come face-to-face with a God who, instead of chasing us, provokes *us* into chasing *him.* While we're bending over sticking our noses into the tomb looking for him, Jesus takes aim and tosses a snowball at our backsides at Easter; and then he runs, hoping that we'll chase him, hoping that we'll enter the pursuit, that we'll go where he's going; he runs, hoping that we'll take the news of resurrection out into a broken, hurting world.

You *did* hear that part of the story, right? The disciples peek into the tomb, but their dead friend is gone. It's not what they had planned; their expectations are turned upside-down. Jesus isn't there; he is on the move. Jesus is on the loose. The angel confirms it, says that if you want to find him, you've got to chase him down, because Jesus has busted out of his stone prison and is loose in the world.

Mark says that Jesus made three appearances after that—three quick, sudden stops. He swings by Mary Magdalene's place, pokes his head inside the door, and says, "Hey, what's up?" But before she can get the coffee warm, he's gone in a blur, off to the country road where two of his friends are walking along, dazed and confused about the horrible events of Friday. He walks with them just long enough to say, "Hey, chin up," before speeding off to see the disciples while they're heating up their TV dinners and wondering what they'll do with the rest of their lives now that their master has bought the farm. He stays just long enough to say, "Go into all the world and proclaim the good news to all creation." And before they know what hit them, he's gone.

Now I never thought I'd say this to my congregation, especially on Easter Sunday, but my job as a preacher is to tell the truth. So the simple truth that I want to get into your complex heads is that if you came looking for Jesus this morning, I've got some bad news—*he is not here!* That's the undeniable mystery of Easter that few preachers would dare admit, because if it's true, then it may mean that you may be in the wrong place right now. It may mean that all I can do for you this morning, like the young man in the white robe at the tomb, is point to where he might have gone. *He is not here*. That's what the gospel says. He *was* here, but he busted loose. The religious people *had* him for a little while; they boxed him in, locked him up, did everything they could do to contain him and make him conform to their own religious structures. They nailed him to the cross, locked him in a tomb, threw away the key. But Jesus busted loose. He's out there in the world, doing his thing. And if you want to find him, you're going to have to chase him down.

Over the years, so much of organized religion has imprisoned the risen Jesus, tamed him, put him in a cage in order to have some kind of proof that he really did rise up from the dead. Poor Jesus. He's not the elusive, cosmic Savior he intended to be; he's "Buddy Jesus," raised from the dead to take care of our petty, private needs. Go to some churches on Easter, and you'll see what I mean. You'll hear a sermon on "The Eight Easter Secrets to Financial Freedom," right? Or, "The Six Keys to Unlocking Your Emotional Tomb." Is this church, you ask, or is this just another Tony Robbins workshop? Or you might hear the preacher give you five irrefutable proofs of the resurrection that will surely convince you that all of this resurrection stuff really is true. Poor Jesus. He's been reduced to propositions and proofs by the very people he rose from the dead to free. But on Easter, I hear him saying to us, "You mean to tell me I went to hell and back for this? I rose from the dead for this? For this? No way. Nice try."

I received this cute little packet in the mail this week from a megachurch in my neighborhood. I suppose it was a creative marketing attempt to lure me into church. The packet contained poppy seeds; it said something like, "Come to life at Easter." Poppy seeds, of all things. Maybe I missed that part of the Easter narrative; I don't recall the gardening motif. I hear Jesus saying, "Poppy seeds? Is this the best you can do? I rose from the dead for poppy seeds?"

Jesus is on the run. Can you blame him? Easter is larger than we want it to be. It's bigger than me, bigger than my success, my financial freedom, my emotional needs, my need for physical proof. Jesus has busted loose from all that. Easter is cosmic. Jesus is on the run.

But Jesus breaks free today. He finds a crack in the walls we've created to contain him, and he slips loose. He crawls through pain and death and absolute darkness in order to break free, not only for you and me but also for the world. And today he is out there. The truth is out there. And the proof of his resurrection, if any can be found, has to be encountered out there in the world if it is to have any significance in our life right here.

The truth *is* out there. The question at Easter is whether we'll go there with him. Will we chase him? Because if we will, then we, too, will be free. If we're on the move with him, chasing him down, throwing ourselves at him, aiming, diving, as Dillard says, then yes, we too are free, because when you pursue the things from above, when you set your mind and strength on the God who is always before you, above your own personal, private needs, then you, too, have been liberated from the dark, cold tombs of this world. You, too, are on the move, pursuing life.

Have you seen that commercial for a certain wireless communications company? I won't mention the name of the company, but the advertising hook is brilliant. A single man, in various places throughout the world, repeats into his cell phone over and over again the simple line: "Can you hear me now? Good...Can you hear me now? Good." That's Jesus at Easter.

He is on the move, and the people who believe in him are chasing him. They are not stuck, fixed in time and space. They are out there, on the move, in pursuit of the one who lobs snowballs at our otherwise self-absorbed, distracted lives and provokes us to chase him to the ends of the earth.

Bono, lead singer for the resilient Irish rock band U2, is someone on the move, someone in hot pursuit of the God who is on the loose in the world. He'd be the first to admit that he is no Saint Francis. But he believes God is on the move in the world, and he's chasing him.

In a single week, Bono appears on the dais at the annual meeting of the World Economic Forum, partnering with Bill Gates for the advocacy of the poor in Third World countries, for relief efforts to AIDS victims across the African continent. A few days later, he's onstage before a TV audience of 130 million viewers for the Super Bowl halftime show, singing "Allelu, Allelu-u-u-ia..." Before the week is over, he's meeting with Treasury Secretary Paul O'Neill on Third World debt relief, and he has meetings with Pope John Paul II, Colin Powell, Jesse Helms still on his schedule. In his spare time, he sits in a bar in New York eating dinner and hanging out with his bandmates and the people he loves. Is he on the move? In word and in deed, he is on the move. "I know it aches/and your heart it breaks/and you can only take so much/ Walk on." The words of someone on the move, right? "Walk on." The alternative, as he sings in another song, is to get "stuck in a moment and you can't get out of it."

In a recent interview with *Time Magazine*, Bono spoke the words that, in the end, speak to the truth we proclaim at Easter. "When you sing, you make people vulnerable to change in their lives. You make yourself vulnerable to change in your life. But in the end, you've got to become the change you want to see in the world."[2]

As we continue to seek out God's promise in the face of the senseless violence and tragedy of September 11, there is good news. Jesus is not here; he is out there, where the world needs him, in the rubble of human tragedy, in the crucible of life. He is on the move. He has become the change he wants to see in the world, and he pokes his head in this little church today, just long enough to see who's up for the chase, because he longs for company, he longs for all of us to become the change he wants to see in the world. Are you ready to go where he is going? Are you ready to look for him, pursue him, when you leave this place today? He is out there. Those with eyes, he says, "See"; those with ears, "Hear." The truth is out there. "I am the way, the truth, and the life," he says, "and I am out there."

I want you to look for him. He's sitting in a wheelchair at the local nursing home right now, lined up with all the rest of the forgotten ones; perched in front of the TV, watching *The Price Is Right* and *Bonanza* reruns, hanging out with the people he loves, the ones he called blessed. You have to look for him. But he's there. Are you willing to go where Jesus goes?

He's out there today, at Union Rescue Mission in downtown L.A., standing in line waiting for his ham sandwich and hot cup of coffee and new pair of shoes. He's there, in the midst of the wandering, houseless ones. You have to look for him, but he's there. Are you willing to go where Jesus goes?

He's out there today, in the cubicle next to yours at the office. He's there when you pass by him, hoping you'll ask him how his day is going, how his family is getting along, how the chemo is going. You've got to look for him, but he's there.

He's in your SUV right now, sitting in the back seat of your Ford Excessive, waiting for you to climb in and head home, hoping you'll answer him when he says, "Hey, buddy, you got a minute? Can we talk? It's been a while."

He's at home right now, your home, sitting back in your easy chair watching the NBA on NBC, waiting for you to come home from church so he can ask you if he can stay a while this time.

He's across the street at the sports bar, sitting in a booth with the middle-aged man who just lost his job in the recent wave of tech layoffs; he's pushing a shopping cart at Sixth and Main in Santa Ana in the guise of an old, tired woman; he's batting seventh on your son's Little League team; he's playing tetherball up at the

Boys' Home in the canyon. He's become the change he longs to see in the world, and he's recruiting today.

He's out there. The truth is out there. He's loose in the world; he's loosed *on* the world. And he's lobbing snowballs at you right now, taking aim, hoping to nail you, finally, to egg you on, to provoke you just enough to commit to the chase, to point yourself, forget yourself, aim, and dive.

The truth is out there. And thanks be to God he is. Open the door, take a long, deep breath, and run.

ART GALLERY

Major Motion Picture Clips

Shawshank Redemption (1994) is the fictional tale of Andy Dufresne (Timothy Robbins), a taciturn banker who is sentenced to two consecutive life terms for a horrible crime that only he knows he didn't commit. While serving hard time at Shawshank Prison, Andy has to learn to get by in the brutal, cutthroat confines of prison life. His quiet strength slowly earns the respect of his fellow inmates—most notably, Red (Morgan Freeman)—and even much of the prison staff. But Andy's seemingly stoic acceptance of his unjust imprisonment hides a fierce determination for freedom.

In this clip, Andy escapes his prison cell through a hole in the wall, concealed for years by a large provocative poster of Rita Hayworth. Crawling through the sewage system, Andy earns his freedom as the rain pours down on him. This dramatic scene includes a single explicit word that can be easily edited or muted for the worship experience. The clip is used in this sermon after establishing the Easter imagery of Jesus' escape from the prisons we've built to contain him. *(VHS, 1:57:00–2:00:16) Total time: 3:16.*

Pop Music

Collective Soul, "Run"

Longing to find the "messenger," the antidote to "boredom," and seeking to find deliverance from "a world of purchase," the narrator confesses that he has "a long way to run."

U2, "Where the Streets Have No Name"

In the words of Bono, the song touches on the theme "of wanting to run, wanting to give in to the urge of the hunter. I always think there are two modes—hunter and protector. Or for me there is anyway. If I gave in to one I'd be an animal. And if I gave in to the other, I'd be completely domesticated. Somewhere between the two is where I live."[3]

Images

Prison cell, iron gates left ajar, an open road in the desert, the earth from space.

The Undertaking

Luke 24:1–12

"Why do you look for the living among the dead?" (Luke 24:5b)

Imagine a funeral. The preacher's giving the eulogy. Friends and family are all gathered together. You've got the flowers and the organ music and the engraved marble tombstone. It's a textbook funeral; everything's going smoothly, right up to the time when the "guest of honor" suddenly pops up out of the coffin.

It really happened. A couple of years ago, Talayi George Sogcwe of South Africa decided to fake his death as a test. "I wanted to know what people would say about me when I'm dead," he told a reporter. "I'm satisfied they spoke the truth about me and not lies."[1]

There's nothing like a moving body to ruin a good funeral, right? That's the thing about Easter. The first Easter started off like a textbook funeral, right? Everybody is dealing with their grief just fine. Everybody is just getting around to finally dealing with the reality of Jesus' death. They're all following the standardized mourning rituals, doing their best to get used to the idea of death, when *life* suddenly happens. It's the last thing anyone in their right mind would come to expect. Death has such a way of pulling our strings.

I received some bad news this week. Two things, actually, that sort of hit me hard. First of all, I came across a respectable university study that indicated that the actual percentage of people in the world who will eventually die is still hovering at right around 100 percent. I had been hoping that we were making progress on this, but they did a study and, apparently, there's still no way around it.

So that got me thinking about this rather dead-end topic, about how much time I've still got on the ticker. That led me to a rather peculiar Web site with an unmistakably curious name—deathclock.com. At deathclock.com you can find out the precise date that you, as we say, will buy the farm. You simply type in your date of birth, your gender, and select your mode of life from a menu of four options. Under mode of life, you can select either "normal," "pessimistic," "sadistic," or optimistic." Now it can be argued that under no circumstances would a "normal" person even go to this Web site, but nevertheless, I selected "normal" because I tend to think more highly of myself than perhaps I really should. So I made my selection and clicked the "calculate" button. And now I'm proud to say that I have my date. According to deathclock.com, it's going to be a Monday, which I figure is rather convenient because, after all, Monday is my day off. So you can rest assured that in no way will my checking out interrupt my normal work schedule. Mark it down. According to deathclock.com, I'll buy the farm on Monday, June 2, in the year 2042.

You see what I'm talking about? We are taught to believe that death is an unavoidable fact of life, that someday it will defeat us, that this is all there is, so we spend so much of our lives worrying about it, counting the ticks on the clock, losing time.

But then Easter happens. Life happens. And God says to us, "Who are you going to believe?"

God wants to do with us what He did for Jesus. He wants to raise us up out of the tombs we've crawled into. He wants to draw us out of whatever darkness we're in, and he wants to lead us out into the light. He wants to meet us at the dead ends of our lives and turn us around to face a whole new life.

The women in the story go to the tomb to do the burial deed. But the body is not there. And the angels appear to them and ask the one question we all need to hear at Easter—"Why do you look for the living among the dead?"

We do that, don't we? We look for life in all the dead places of our lives. Like the women who go to the tomb, we look at tragedy or heartbreak or disappointment or dead ends, and we do our best to try to get used to it, to live through it, to take our lumps and swallow hard and do what we can to adjust, adapt, and accept it. Because it's part of life. If it bleeds, they say, it leads. Bad news has a way of doing that to us. We look at life and say, "It is what it is." That's the gospel of our culture. As Christof, in the movie *The Truman Show* puts it, "We accept the reality of the world with which we are presented." That is the gospel of our culture. But it is not the gospel of Jesus Christ.

Easter is divine defiance, God's cosmic refusal to accept and adjust to the way things are. At Easter, God is too busy trying to get used to the way things should be to settle for what already is.

Reynolds Price, one of North America's great writers, woke up one day several years ago to discover that he had a large tumor on his spine the size of a melon. The surgery left him paralyzed. The radiation left him emotionally and physically exhausted. He fell into a deep depression. His life, his family, his career, his faith—all nearly destroyed. He wrote a book about his journey, about the ways he found healing and strength to rebuild his life and faith. He entitled the book, curiously, *A Whole New Life.* He says that it would have been a great favor to him if someone had walked up to his hospital bed right at the start and said, "Reynolds Price is now dead. Who will you be now?" When bad news strikes, he says, "Have one hard cry, if the tears will come. Then stanch the grief, by whatever legal means. Next find your way to be somebody else, the next viable you—a stripped down, whole other clear-eyed person, realistic as a sawed-off shotgun and thankful for air."[2]

You don't have to wait any longer. You don't have to adjust and adapt and accept life as it is. Unless a seed falls into the earth and dies, it cannot grow, says Jesus. So let it go. Proclaim it dead. Then see what God can do with you, so that you can finally leave this graveyard behind.

God seeks to undertake a miracle in our life today. A dead faith, sealed in the tomb of disappointment and doubt, can live again. A dead relationship, sealed in the tomb of misunderstanding, pride, betrayal, or hurt, can live again. A dead spirit, sealed in the tomb of wrongdoing and regret and sin, can live again. Whatever seems lost, ruined, abandoned, or broken—it can be restored. You can either get used to it, or you can pronounce it dead and give it to God to raise it up and give it new life.

Every Christian has a graveyard in his life. Every Christian has disappointment, grief, sorrow, and tragedy buried deep in the soil of her soul. But the question at Easter is this: How many used tombstones are you ready to put up for sale?

In 1995, at the age of twenty-five, Lance Armstrong was the greatest cyclist in North America. Then, almost at once, his career, and his very life, was nearly derailed by a diagnosis of advanced testicular cancer. The cancer had traveled to his brain and his lungs. At the time, his doctors gave him a 3 percent chance of survival.

Two years later, after countless surgeries and constant

treatments of radiation and chemotherapy, Lance Armstrong climbed back on his bike and began the slow ascent back into life. The world had forgotten about Lance Armstrong, until he took the yellow jersey at the first stage of the 1999 Tour de France and never gave it up. Three weeks and 2,200 miles later, Lance Armstrong won the most grueling sporting event ever conceived.

He writes about the challenges of climbing the steep Alps of the Tour and reflecting on his own life.

> As I rode upward, I reflected on my life, back to all points, my childhood, my early races, my illness, and how it changed me. Maybe it was the primitive act of climbing that made me confront the issues I'd been evading for weeks. It was time to quit stalling, I realized. *Move,* I told myself...
>
> As I continued upward, I saw my life as a whole. I saw the pattern and the privilege of it, and the purpose of it, too. It was simply this: I was meant for a long, hard climb.[3]

> In those first days after crossing the finish line in Paris I was swept up in a wave of attention, and as I struggled to keep things in perspective, I asked myself why my victory had such a profound effect on people. Maybe it's because illness is universal—we've all been sick, no one is immune—and so winning the Tour was a symbolic act, proof that you can not only survive cancer, but thrive after it. Maybe, as my friend Phil Knight says, I am hope.[4]

> We each cope differently with the specter of our own deaths. Some people deny it. Some people pray. Some numb themselves with tequila. I was tempted to do a little of each of those things. But I think we are supposed to try to face it straightforwardly, armed with nothing but courage. The definition of courage is: the quality of spirit that enables one to encounter danger with firmness and without fear."[5]

That courage is ours at Easter, given to us by a defiant God who refuses to do it any other way. God wants to do with us what God did with Jesus, and today, he does it. So "put away your former way of life, your old self, corrupt and deluded by its lusts, and...be renewed in the spirit of your minds, and...clothe yourselves with the new self, created according to the likeness of God in true righteousness and holiness" (Eph. 4:22–24).

ART GALLERY

Major Motion Picture Clips

In *The Truman Show* (1998), the life of Truman Burbank (Jim Carrey) has been broadcast around the world with tremendous success since the very day he was born. A star for the mere fact that he exists, Truman has no idea that there are cameras in every corner of his world. Over time, he begins to see that his entire life has been staged, that his wife and friends are mere actors, that even the sun is "cued."

This scene leads viewers to the dramatic conclusion to the movie, and to the television show, when Truman boards a small sailboat with the intention of leaving the island and establishing a new life. After surviving a violent, "cued" storm, Truman's boat crashes into the invisible paper wall of the huge geodesic dome that contains him, and Truman climbs the steps and prepares to walk out the door. Truman's dialogue with Christof, his "creator," reminds us that often those who claim to love us are those who seek to use us for their own purposes. While Christof urges Truman to adjust and accept his world, Truman longs for freedom from it. *(VHS, 1:28:00–1:35:12) Total time: 7:12.*

Pop Music

Collective Soul, "Heaven's Already Here"

Having found a love that lights the way, there is no more need to live in darkness. It's a new morning, the dawning of peace of mind and heaven on earth.

U2, "Beautiful Day"

Described by the band as a hymn, the Grammy-winning song points to hope, vindication, beauty, and healing for the one who knows he's "not a hopeless case."

Images

Lance Armstrong on the bike, coffins, open caves, tombstones, and cemeteries.

To Infinity and Beyond

Acts 2:1–21

> *And suddenly from heaven there came a sound like the rush of a violent wind, and it filled the entire house where they were sitting. Divided tongues, as of fire, appeared among them, and a tongue rested on each of them. All of them were filled with the Holy Spirit. (Acts 2:2–4a)*

Do you ever "do the Dew"? I do the Dew, do you? Not that I recommend doing the Dew—it's got more caffeine than a venti café mocha and more sugar than a C&H silo, which means that if you super-size your Dew at the drive thru, you'll no doubt have enough energy to put your pet octopus to bed. Mountain Dew is to soda what octane is to gas, right? It should be a controlled substance if you ask me.

Have you ever seen the commercials for the neon green Dew? They're exhausting. A man chases down a cheetah in the jungle just to get his stolen Dew back—"Bad kitty," he says. Another commercial has a guy head-butting a ram in the wilderness over a Dew. Or my personal favorite—the mock opera version of Queen's "Bohemian Rhapsody," in which the actors sing,

> I see a little silhouette of a can
> Mountain Dew Mountain Dew time to do the slamdango...
>
> They're just thirsty dudes anybody knows that
> They're just thirsty dudes out on a thirsty day
> Sparing their life from this banality.

Think about it—a soft drink is sparing some thirsty dudes from "this banality." Their lives were going nowhere, right? Until they found the Dew. They didn't even have to come forward for an altar call or contribute to the building fund. They found the Dew, and it gave them a reason to keep living.

It's like that old Dreyer's brand ice cream commercial from a few years back, with that little baby sitting there on the floor, bored stiff, with not a thing in the world to do. Mom comes in with the groceries and calls the baby into the kitchen for some ice cream, but he doesn't budge, right? Big deal; it doesn't even phase him. "It's Dreyer's," she says, and suddenly the baby busts a move on the living room floor, break dancing and moon walking and buzzing around like, you know, like real babies do. The moment I saw that commercial, I told Lori, "Keep that ice cream away from the kids."

Give it a try sometime. Watch the advertisements closely for the underlying message they sell, and you'll find that most of them say the same thing: Life is pretty boring and mediocre and uneventful without our product. Listen to the slogans—"Get out of the old; get into the cold," or "Life's too short; play hard," or "Life's a sport; drink it up," or simply, "Zoom, zoom, zoom"—all of which seem to suggest that we *are* "into the old," "not playing hard enough," "not drinking up enough life," or that there's just not enough "zoom" in our lives. So we're supposed to buy these products, they say, because the last thing we want to do is lead boring, mediocre, uneventful lives.

And then we become mediocre with style, right? Studies show that we're still pretty boring, mediocre, and uneventful—even if we do buy these products. I read this week that over the last ten years, 90 percent of all athletic shoes we purchased never saw a single exercise session. Their biggest use? Looking good at the mall.

Today is Pentecost, the fiftieth day after Easter. In a strange sense, it is the birthday of the church. It is the day that Christians got a taste of their spiritual dew for the first time and really started living the kind of life that Jesus told them to live before he left this earth.

The scene is set in Jerusalem, where the followers of Jesus are gathered together in one place, doing what some churches do quite well—they're having committee meetings, hanging around doing absolutely nothing important, debating on how much to spend on the new carpet and what color the new toilet seat should be. Their best days are behind them—the days when they had a real leader named Jesus. Now it's enough just to hold the line and keep the lights on. The doors are locked, and that's just fine. No need to go public with things, or rock the boat with new people who might have new ideas or different agendas from ours. In fact, we already have too many of those people in here, they thought, but that's all right, because we're not talking to them anyway. It was your ordinary, mediocre, uneventful, boring church, where people leave the place looking as dead and bored and straight-faced as they did when they entered.

But then it happens. In all that boredom and mediocrity, God shows up. The floor begins to shake violently; the drapes are blown off the windows; a deafening noise explodes through the silence and deadness of that place; and in an instant, their little living room is transformed into something like a nuclear reactor, with enough unharnessed power to light the world ten times over. And all the bickering, all the boredom, all the mediocrity fades away. Someone laughs; another starts to preach; another bows her head and starts to pray. It felt like the old days when Jesus was with them, only different. He wasn't there; but it felt like he was. So they started talking to one another again; they started praying with one another again, telling stories, making plans, talking about the future, preaching, and reminding one another of what Jesus said to them—the things they hadn't done for quite some time.

I like what Luke does here. He says that all this commotion woke up the neighbors; they gather around the house in their slippers and pajamas, peeking through the windows, assessing the situation. "What's up with the Jesus people?" someone asks. And someone replies, "Oh, they're just drunk. Too much Dew."

But they are not filled with wine, or dew, or anything else that can be bought or sold. They are filled with the Holy Spirit, says Peter, and that means that it's time for the young to see visions and the old to dream dreams, and it's time for us to claim our purpose and live for Christ. This is the story of Pentecost.

Pentecost is the day that we celebrate every year to remind ourselves that God wants more out of us than we are giving him. It reminds us that God is not impressed with whatever mediocrity we're giving him. God's standards are higher than our efforts. If you're bored with your life, if your life is just ordinary and mediocre and uninteresting, it's not God's fault. He's given you the power of the Holy Spirit to dream dreams and see visions and walk in faith; he's given you the promise that with this power you cannot be defeated.

Søren Kierkegaard, the great existentialist of the nineteenth century, used to tell the story about the duck preacher and the duck church. Every Sunday, all the ducks would waddle into church, quacking and flopping all the way to the pews. They'd sit down and sing duck songs, quack out a few hymns, until the duck preacher stood up to give the sermon. The duck preacher, every week, would tell the ducks in his congregation that they didn't have to walk and waddle everywhere, that they could actually fly—that's why they have wings, after all. "All you have to do is flap those wings," he'd tell them. With wings you can mount up and soar like eagles. No walls can confine you! No fences can hold you! You have wings. God has given you wings, and you can fly like birds." The ducks loved that sermon. He told it to them every week. As they listened, they could almost see it in their duck imaginations. When the sermon was over, they'd shout "Amen!" sing one last duck hymn, then waddle out the door, all the way home.

Remember Buzz Lightyear? Buzz is a great caricature of the spiritual life. Buzz shows up one day as a birthday gift to a child. He is a toy, but he doesn't know it. All the other toys, such as Woody, Ham, Potato Head, Slinky, and Little Bo Peep have come to grips with their purpose in life—they know they're not real; they know they're toys; they know that their sole purpose in life is to be a companion to the child. But Buzz thinks he's the real thing. He is the perfect up-and-comer, right? He thinks he's the real thing, going to change the world, got the universe on his shoulders. He thinks he can really fly, which is another way of saying he thinks he can do anything, the impossible. He is like the disciples right before Jesus checks out—they are ready to conquer the world.

For a while the illusion works. Most of us can run on illusions for a while. We can deceive ourselves into thinking that we can do anything on our own strength. Buzz proves he can fly, but it's really not flight. It's luck. The problem is that all the other toys, save for Woody, believe that he indeed did fly, supporting the myth, the illusion. We call them codependents in today's world.

But there comes a time in the movie, a crunch-time moment, a moment of truth, in which Buzz is forced to fly, and he fails miserably. *(Show major motion picture clip 1.)*

You can feel his anguish and heartbreak when he leaps off the stairs and, in mid-flight, realizes he is not flying, but falling, and falling fast. You can see the expression on his face—the fear, panic, dejection. He's a complete mess. Some people call that mid-life crisis, I believe—the realization that your dreams of changing the world, of making something of yourself, were unrealistic and unreachable and you feel a sense of failure setting in. He is not what he always envisioned himself to be, which is the very thing that affects that early church in Jerusalem just before Pentecost. It's seemingly all downhill from here. We'll resign to the mediocrity, boredom, uneventfulness of life as long as that means we don't have to face the truth of our own lives. If I can't fly, then what can I do?

But you'll remember how the story ends. Buzz experiences redemption, in a sense. He pulls his life together when he finally owns up to his created purpose in life: to become a companion to a child. But now even that is in jeopardy. He's been separated from the child. He may never get back. It will take a miracle for him to chase down the moving van and fulfill his purpose. *(Show major motion picture clip 2.)*

This is Pentecost, friends. When we are finally powered not by our own illusions or delusions or myths or self-deceptions—when we finally give up our overbearing need to control, our fear of failure, our aversion to taking risks, our grip on mediocrity, and our need to maintain stability—and give in to the unpredictable and resilient Spirit of God, which is powerful enough to take us to infinity and beyond.

The truth, as Buzz reminds us while holding on to the rocket in mid-air, is honest and humble: "I'm not flying...This is falling, with style."

This is my Pentecost prayer for you and me and for this church. That we would claim and claim again our purpose in life, give up the illusions that keep us from a life lived in the Spirit, accept that God is God and we are not, and admit that, while we cannot fly, we do have this match, given by our God, to light this rocket, to risk falling for the hope of soaring in God's holy kingdom.

ART GALLERY

Major Motion Picture Clips

Clip 1: *Toy Story* (1995). A little boy's toys are thrown into chaos when a new Space Ranger arrives to compete for supremacy with the boy's old favorite (a wooden cowboy). When the feuding toys become lost, they are forced to set aside their differences to get home.

In this scene, Buzz attempts the great escape from the house of doom by jumping from the top of the staircase and attempting to fly out the door, only to crash and burn. Play clip as noted in sermon. *(VHS, 45:45–48:27) Total time: 2:42.*

Clip 2: *Toy Story* (1995). Woody and Buzz work together to be reunited with the child. When the match is extinguished by the breeze of a passing car, Woody uses Buzz's plastic space helmet to reflect the sunlight and light the rocket fuse. The rocket ignites, and Buzz and Woody soar through the air, landing in the child's box of toys in the backseat of the car. Use clip as noted in sermon. *(VHS, 1:10:45–1:14:55) Total time: 4:10.*

Pop Music

Collective Soul, "Breathe"

Seeing love and passion dissolve, a man resolves to plant seeds, shed light, start singing, and breathe a little love. "Yeah, I'm gonna take a deep breath for you/Come on now people/Come on now breathe..."

Images

Rocket with a fuse, flames, a burning match.

Don't Do the Math

Matthew 18:21–35

Then Peter came and said to him, "Lord, if another member of the church sins against me, how often should I forgive? As many as seven times?" Jesus said to him, "Not seven times, but, I tell you, seventy-seven times." (Matthew 18:21–22)

When I pulled myself out of bed Thursday morning, it was like any other ordinary day, nothing particularly unusual. The sun peered through the east window in the bedroom as it had every morning for the previous five years, spilling a triangle of sunlight onto the far end of the bed, where the cat lay contented, like a king on his throne. I could hear the familiar sounds of neighbors turning over the engines of their cars, of dogs debating with each other through the fence, of sprinklers popping up next door, as if they all had held their breath all night. There was nothing to signal any strange diversion from the ordinary morning routine; everything was in its place; nothing was unusual, save a feeling—a hunch, perhaps—that something was now here, which I had never before noticed.

I stood at the sink to brush my teeth and shave, and I could feel it then—something near, yet elusive; something that sounded like something trying not to make a sound; something gazing at me, hidden in plain view. I asked Lori if she could feel it too. She said, "Mark, there's a pill for things like this."

I sent the kids off to school, got dressed, grabbed my briefcase, and made my way out the door—and still that hunch, that uneasiness you get when you know something is not normal but can't for the life of you put a finger on it. I could feel it following me, first around the house, then down the stairs, through the door, along the walkway.

I felt it climb into the car with me. And when I looked in the rearview mirror, there it was, there *they* were, both of them, sitting in the backseat, all buckled in and ready to go for a ride.

"Who are you?" I asked.

The one on the right said, "Mark, we've been through this a hundred times. You ask the same question every morning. I thought we were friends."

"Tell me again," I asked. "What's your name? I can't recall."

"Justice," he said with a huff.

"And you," I said to the one on the left. "I'm sorry, but I don't remember your name either."

"It's all right," she said with a kind smile. "My name is Mercy."

Justice and Mercy, sitting right there in my back seat.

"Why are you here?" I asked.

Justice didn't hesitate. "To look out for you," he said, "because it's a hard world out there, and without me, people will trample you."

I glanced at Mercy, who waited, as always, for Justice to finish. She said, "I'm here to show you how to look out for somebody other than yourself, because it's a hard world out there, and without me, you'll trample people."

We talked for a while as I made the familiar drive to the office. It turns out that Mercy and Justice have been with me every day of my life; they go everywhere I go, see everything I see, know me through and through. And they get along amazingly well, considering they are so unlike each other. Justice has the pectorals of Arnold Schwarzenegger and the jawline of Clint Eastwood. Mercy has the seductive glow of Alanis Morissette and the soft, trusting face of Victor French, without the beard.

Heading down Antonio Parkway, a middle-aged man driving a Ford Excursion pulls out in front of me, causing me to brake suddenly. Mercy and Justice bump their noses on the backs of the seats in front of them and gasp for air. Justice leans forward, puts his hand on my shoulder, and says with a certain disbelief, "You gonna just take that, Mark? That guy's got some serious issues. Someone needs to send him a message."

Justice has a point. Someone has to teach this guy a lesson. An errant Excursion is a suburban weapon of mass destruction. Without Justice, chaos is loosed in the world.

Mercy waits for Justice to have his say, as she always does. "That guy's got some serious issues, Mark" she says, "Just like you. Let it go."

Justice leans back, shakes his head, folds his arms in frustration. Sometimes Justice wins. Sometimes Mercy. I hear them out, every moment of every day. But they always give me the freedom to choose between the two.

They're with me all day. They are inseparable. Justice is part of my human nature; Mercy, my Christian nature. I struggle between the two. Both are good friends, but I will tell you a secret about me: It's my nature to want to let Justice have his way with me.

When the homeless man walks in and asks me for twenty dollars to buy a new pair of shoes, Justice asks me if he deserves it; Mercy asks me if I deserve the shoes on my own feet.

When I stand at the bedside of a woman whose body is riddled with cancer, Justice whispers in my ear, "She doesn't deserve this, not her"; Mercy whispers in the other, "No one deserves this."

When someone takes an unfair, cruel shot at me, Justice says, "Never forget it"; Mercy says, "Remember who you are."

When someone provokes me, Justice says, "Stand your ground"; Mercy says, "Blessed are the peacemakers."

When someone hurts me, Justice says, "An eye for an eye"; Mercy says, "Turn the other cheek."

Justice keeps an eye on his enemies; Mercy prays for them. Justice packs a piece of chalk in his pocket to keep score of rights and wrongs; Mercy carries an eraser to wipe them all away. Justice is a realist; Mercy, an idealist. Justice is a lion; Mercy, a lamb.

Have you ever met them? Do they ride in your backseat? Or does Justice, more often than not, ride shotgun?

If you are like me, like Peter in the story from Matthew's gospel this morning, these two characters rent little loft apartments in your head and throw loud parties when you lie down to go to sleep at night. You pull the covers up to your chin and think back on the events of the day—the news in the world, the people in your life—and that's when the voices are heard. Who wronged me; who did I wrong? Who did good to me, and what do I owe them for it? Who stabbed me in the back, and how will I respond?

Matthew asks Jesus, "How many times do I have to forgive someone who does me wrong? Is seven times a pretty fair limit on the forgiveness barometer?" And Jesus throws out this wild number: "not seven, Pete, but seventy-seven times."

It's a strange figure, isn't it—seventy-seven times? At first glance, you might think his point is that by the time you get past twelve or thirteen, you'll begin to lose count, right? And that *is* part of his point. Don't bother doing the math, right? But there is more here, as there always is with Jesus. He goes beyond the practical advice and offers some pretty sound teaching here.

The reference to "seventy-seven times" goes all the way back to the book of Genesis, the first book in the Old Testament. You go to chapter four of that book, and you meet a guy by the name of Lamech. Lamech is the fifth generation of Cain's family. You remember Cain, right? Cain did away with his brother Abel in the fields somewhere outside of paradise, the garden of Eden.

Cain was the first murderer in human history according to the biblical story. And his murderous instinct was passed on from generation to generation. Lamech inherited Cain's thirst for justice through the shedding of blood. In chapter four, Lamech is sitting in his easy chair, watching the NFL on Fox, when out of the blue he announces to his household, "If Cain is avenged sevenfold, then Lamech is avenged seventy-sevenfold" (Gen. 4:24, paraphrased) In other words, there is no limit on the number of heads that will roll should anyone do me wrong. And in that statement, the law of endless retribution and revenge is encoded in the DNA of humanity forever.

If we are all children of Adam, as the Bible suggests, then we are all brothers and sisters of Lamech, whose blood flows through us, whose thirst for justice has no limits. Lamech practiced the third law of thermodynamics before Newton ever discovered it: For every action there is an equal and opposite reaction. Every mushroom cloud, every school yard fight, every weapon of mass destruction, every domestic battering is one more factor in the endless formula of seventy-seven.

I know what you're thinking. I often find myself thinking the same, that there is a difference between thirsting for blood and hungering for justice, a clear distinction between getting revenge and holding your ground. But I am not convinced; there are some who would disagree: the family of the seventeen-year-old Buena Park boy, Brandon Ketsdever, who was shot and killed for attempting to steal a Halloween pumpkin decoration from a neighbor's yard four years ago. They might beg to differ. Or the dozens—no, hundreds—of dead women and children in the villages of Afghanistan who, despite their innocence in the war against terror, are too dead to argue the point. Or the more than one hundred wrongfully convicted prisoners released from prison, many of them from death row, after having been proven innocent on grounds of DNA evidence by the nationwide Innocence Project.

They might have something to say about it. The truth about you and me is that while there is often a clear line between revenge and justice, we too often fail to see it and grow too accustomed to the occasionally merciless, often murderous, imprecision of justice.

We hold our grudges too long; we stockpile our injuries and use them as weapons. One act of indiscretion against us too often equals a *seventy-sevenfold* repayment.

But leave it to Jesus to take that formula of seventy-seven, draw a line underneath it, and divide it by the single factor of his own life and blood, so that every time we do the math in order to arrive at justice, it always equals mercy, seventy-sevenfold.

Jesus does the math for us, so that we don't have to. His mercy *is* his justice, and our calling as Christians is to live in the condition of that mercy and pay it forward, even if it puts us in debt according to the standards of justice in this world.

Don't expect it to make sense. It won't make sense. Mercy never does. That's why it's rare, and yet so revolutionary.

In the riots that followed the first Rodney King verdict, Reginald Denny was dragged from his truck and brutally beaten by a raging mob in downtown Los Angeles. It was captured on video; the images were as shocking and violent as the beating of Rodney King months earlier. For the mob, it was justice, seventy-sevenfold. For Reginald Denny, it became an opportunity to do some holy math. After his painful recovery, Denny met face-to-face with his attackers, shook hands with them, and publicly forgave them. A reporter who witnessed that profoundly moving scene later commented about what he saw. He wrote, "It is believed that Reginald Denny is suffering from brain damage."[1]

It doesn't make sense to the world; it rarely makes sense to most Christians. But it is the way of Jesus, the only way of Jesus; and according to the parable Jesus tells, it's a requirement for life in the kingdom of God.

How many times, asks Peter? And Jesus tells him a story about a man who, after having his own debt forgiven, can't bring himself to pay it forward by forgiving his own debtor, and in so doing excludes himself from a life lived under the condition of mercy and the inheritance of the kingdom of God. The man chose justice, was judged by the master accordingly, and was found wanting.

Why seventy-seven? Maybe Jesus understood that it takes seventy-seven times to undo our need to settle the score, to untrain ourselves of the ways of retribution, to decondition our natural response to injustice, to detox from our thirst for blood. Maybe he set the standard so high because he understood that the first time would spark something in us—a revolution, an irrevocable conversion, a relentless protest against the curse of Lamech, the formula of seventy-seven. He knew that just once is a start for you and me and a victory for the kingdom of God.

In the movie *Pay It Forward,* Helen Hunt's character gets to that point in her life when she knows she must forgive her mother for the deep pain she caused in her life. She has met face-to-face with mercy in her life and now seeks to pay it forward in the world, beginning with the person in her life who needs it the most. *(Show major motion picture clip.)*

There is considerable freedom in such moments. It comes not from evening the score, but erasing it altogether and starting over. And it begins by coming face-to-face with the one who forgives us, who says, "Go and do likewise."

I want you to take Justice and Mercy for a ride this week. Take them first to a little hill near the trash heap just outside of town, a place on the map called Golgotha, where one sinless man hangs between two criminals, surrounded by a mob of the children of Lamech. Listen carefully to the man in the middle who whispers, "Father, forgive them," as he breathes in all the violence hurled at him and holds it in until what finally comes out is the breath of mercy, holy and pure. He is abused but will not retaliate. Condemned, but will not judge, beaten seventy-seven times but willing to forgive seventy-seven times more. Take Justice and Mercy there, because in witnessing that place, that act, that man, the two—Justice and Mercy—become one. At the cross, God's mercy *becomes* God's justice, and they take on a single name—Grace.

Then climb back in the car and go home, taking Grace there with you. Let Grace ride shotgun the whole way. Show Grace where you live, and invite Grace to stay. Take Grace into your living room, your kids' bedrooms, your master suite. Take Grace next door, to the office, to the soccer fields, and to the supermarket. Take Grace into the loft apartments of your head at midnight, when you find yourself tallying up the score of the day. And when the sun peeks through the east window in the morning, and when you climb back in your car, look into the rearview mirror and ask the one sitting there this simple question: "What's your name?"

He will say, with a kind smile, "Jesus."

ART GALLERY

Major Motion Picture Clips

Pay It Forward (2000) is a heartwarming tale about an eleven-year-old boy, Trevor McKinney, who comes up with a utopian idea as a project for school. Trevor's history teacher, Eugene Simenot (Kevin Spacey), offers the same ongoing extra-credit assignment he gives to students every year: Come up with an idea that will change the world. Trevor dreams up a stunning scheme: that every person who benefits from someone else's good deed should "pay it forward," instead of paying it back, and in turn offer favors to three other people.

The recommended scene finds Trevor's mother, played by Helen Hunt, meeting up with her homeless, alcoholic mother in a squatter's camp outside of town. Recalling her painful past as a child of an alcoholic, single mother, she tells her mother, "I forgive you." *(VHS 1:42:51–1:46:15) Total time: 3:24.*

Pop Music

Don Henley, "Forgiveness"

The narrator offers a word of forgiveness to a lover from his past—"forgiveness...even if you don't love me anymore."

Images

Math or physics formulas, pictures of Arnold Schwarzenegger and Clint Eastwood, pictures of a face gazing into a rearview mirror.

Notes

Introduction

[1]Annie Dillard, *The Writing Life* (New York: HarperPerennial, 1989), 68.

[2]For a thoughtful, compelling interpretation of GenX spirituality, including these and other themes, see Tom Beaudoin, *Virtual Faith: The Irreverent Spiritual Quest of Generation X* (San Francisco: Jossey-Bass, 1998).

From Shame to Sheep

[1]See Geoffrey Holtz, *Welcome to the Jungle: The Why behind Generation X* (New York: St. Martin's Griffin, 1995).

[2]See Neil Howe and Bill Strauss, *13th Gen: Abort, Retry, Ignore, Fail?* (New York: Vintage Books, 1993).

[3]David Hilfiker, *Not All of Us Are Saints: A Doctor's Journey with the Poor* (New York: Hill and Wang, 1994), 248.

[4]David Rosenberg, "Psalm 23," in *A Poet's Bible: Rediscovering the Voices of the Original Text* (New York: Hyperion, 1991), 19–20.

[5]Dietrich Bonhoeffer, *Letters and Papers from Prison* (New York: Macmillan, 1953), 347–48.

How Not to Do the Right Thing

[1]Larry Lauden, *The Book of Risks: Fascinating Facts about the Chances We Take Everyday* (New York: John Wiley and Sons, 1994).

[2]Mary Ann Bird, "The Whisper Test," published online at http:www.thechristianwall.org/seven_words.htm.

Take the Long Way Home

[1]John Dear, S.J., "The Solitary Witness of Franz Jagerstatter," *Sojourners Magazine* 22, no. 7 (August 1993): 7.

[2]William Butler Yeats, "The Maji," *Selected Poems and Three Plays* (New York: Collier Books, 1986), 49.

[3]Thomas Lynch, *Bodies in Motion and at Rest: On Metaphor and Mortality* (New York: W.W. Norton, 2000), 107–9.

[4]Niall Stokes, *Into the Heart: The Stories behind the Music* (New York: Thunder's Mouth Press, 2002), 151.

Incite Hope

[1]Walter Wink, *Engaging the Powers: Discernment and Resistance in a World of Domination* (Minneapolis: Fortress Press, 1992), 13–31.

[2]Dietrich Bonhoeffer, *Letters and Papers from Prison* (New York: Macmillan, 1953), 139–43.

[3]*The United Methodist Book of Worship* (Nashville: United Methodist Publishing House, 1992), 425–26.

[4]Terry Mattingly, "Rock Star Tries to Ease Third World Plight," *Good News Magazine* (Sept/Oct 2001). Archived at www.goodnewsmag.org.

The Sound of Sheer Silence

[1]Frederick Buechner, *Telling Secrets: A Memoir* (New York: HarperCollins, 1991), 49–50.

[2]Lawrence Kushner, *God Was in This Place and I, I Did Not Know* (Woodstock, Vt.: Jewish Lights, 1991), 97.

[3]T. S. Eliot, "Ash Wednesday" in *The Complete Poems and Plays* (New York: Harcourt Brace, 1952), 65.

Daily Bread

[1]For a compelling critique of contemporary consumerism, and helpful suggestions for resistance, see Juliet B. Schor, *The Overspent American: Upscaling, Downshifting, and the New Consumer* (New York: Basic Books, 1998).

[2]John Francis Kavanaugh, *Following Christ in a Consumer Society: The Spirituality of Cultural Resistance* (New York: Orbis Books, 1981), 47.

[3]Thomas Lynch, *The Undertaking: Life Studies from the Dismal Trade* (New York: Penguin Books, 1997), 6–7.

Life after God

[1]Fyodor Dostoyevsky, *The Brothers Karamazov* (New York: Penguin Books, 1993), 283–302.

[2]Douglas Coupland, "1000 Years (Life after God)," in *Life after God* (New York: Pocket Books, 1994), 357–60.

[3]Dave Eggers, *A Heartbreaking Work of Staggering Genius* (New York: Simon & Schuster, 2000), 207.

Mile Twenty

[1]Tim Dearborn, *Taste and See: Awakening Our Spiritual Senses* (Downers Grove, Ill.: InterVarsity Press, 1996), 62.

[2]Ibid., 131.

[3]See Tolbert McCarroll, *Morning Glory Babies: Children with AIDS and the Celebration of Life* (New York: St. Martin's Press, 1988).

[4]Anne Lamott, *Operating Instructions: A Journal of My Son's First Year* (New York: Ballantine Books, 1993), 70.

[5]William Styron, *Darkness Visible: A Memoir of Madness,* large print ed. (New York: Random House, 1990), 117–18.

Our Father...

[1]Frederick Buechner, *Whistling in the Dark: An ABC Theologized* (New York: HarperCollins, 1988), 76.

[2]See N. T. Wright, *The Lord and His Prayer* (Grand Rapids: Eerdmans, 1997), 14–15.

[3]J. D. Dolan, *Phoenix: A Brother's Life* (New York: Knopf, 2000), 185–86.

Partly Cloudy, Chance of Rain

[1]Walter Brueggemann, *First and Second Samuel* (Louisville: John Knox Press, 1990), 273.

Ready for Prime Time

[1]George Saunders, "The Falls," in *Pastoralia* (New York: Riverhead Books, 2000), 176–88.

[2]Anne Lamott, *Bird by Bird: Some Instructions on Writing and Life* (New York: Doubleday, 1994), 102.

[3]"Buttprints in the Sand" by Anonymous. Found online at http://www.greaterthings.com/Humor/buttprints.htm.

[4]Fred Craddock, *Craddock Stories* (St. Louis: Chalice Press, 2001), 86.

[5]Emily Dickinson, "492," in *The Poems of Emily Dickinson* (Cambridge, Mass.: Belknap Press, 1999), 224.

[6]Stephen Ambrose, *Undaunted Courage* (New York: Simon & Schuster, 1996), 31.

Enough Is Enough

[1]Anne Lamott, *Traveling Mercies: Some Thoughts on Faith* (New York: Pantheon Books, 1999), 101–2.

Divine Interruptions

[1]Frederick Buechner, *Listening to Your Life: Daily Meditations with Frederick Buechner* (New York: Harper Collins, 1992), 135–36.

No Bull

[1]As reproduced in Leonard Sweet, *Aqua Church: Essential Leadership Arts for Piloting Your Church in Today's Fluid Culture* (Loveland, Colo.: Group, 1999), 259.

The Truth Is Out There

[1]Annie Dillard, *An American Childhood* (New York: Harper and Row, 1987), 46–48.

[2]Josh Tyrangiel, "Bono," *Time* (March 04, 2002). Archived online at www.time.com.

[3]Niall Stokes, *Into the Heart: The Stories behind Every Song* (New York: Thunder Mouth's Press, 2002), 64.

The Undertaking

[1]Talayi George Sogcwe, in "A Tisket, a Tasket, I'm Comin' Outta the Casket!" *Campus Life* (November/December 1997), published online at http://www.christianitytoday.com/cl/7c3/7c3086.html.

[2]Reynolds Price, *A Whole New Life: An Illness and a Healing* (New York: Atheneum, 1994), 183.

[3]Lance Armstrong, *It's Not about the Bike: My Journey Back to Life* (New York: G. P. Putnam's Sons, 2000), 202.

[4]Ibid., 265.

[5]Ibid., 272.

Don't Do the Math

[1]As told by William Willimon.